Rabbi Cindy Enger
Diane Gardsbane
Editors

Domestic Abuse and the Jewish Community: Perspectives from the First International Conference

Domestic Abuse and the Jewish Community: Perspectives from the First International Conference has been co-published simultaneously as *Journal of Religion & Abuse,* Volume 6, Numbers 3 and 4 2004.

Pre-publication
REVIEWS,
COMMENTARIES,
EVALUATIONS . . .

"THE PUBLICATION OF THIS BOOK IS A SIGNIFICANT EVENT. This is a timely collection, one that should grace the bookshelves of rabbis and other communal leaders, as well as those in every Jewish home. The denial and minimization of violence against women and children are well-challenged by the level of openness and clarity found in the many excellent essays in this volume."

Rabbi Robert J. Gluck
Assistant Professor
University of Albany

More Pre-publication
REVIEWS, COMMENTARIES, EVALUATIONS . . .

"UNIQUE . . . A remarkable compendium of diverse faces in the Jewish global community: survivors of domestic violence, rabbis, PhDs, community leaders who keep women's shelters open, academicians, feminists, politicians, and visionaries who want to effect *Tikkun Olam* (repairing the world) on the issue of domestic abuse. The editors of this volume have crafted a single message form the myriad voices of survivors/thrivers and activists alike: we need to spread the word that this kind of abuse will no longer be tolerated, nor can it be religiously justified."

Rabbi Shira Stern, DMin, BCC (Board Certified Chaplain)
Director
The Center for Studies
in Jewish Pastoral Care
The HealthCare Chaplaincy

"Human being are made 'in the image of God' and as such are holy and must be protected. This book shows us that this is not an impossible how this plague is being confronted by making the community aware of the problem and thus preventing domestic violence through education, empowering women to take charge of their lives, and helping victims, including children, rebuild their lives and stop perpetrating the cycle of violence in the next generation."

Rabbi Diana Villa
Research Fellow
The Center for Women
in Jewish Law
The Schechter Institute
of Jewish Studies
Jerusalem, Israel

The Haworth Pastoral Press®
An Imprint of The Haworth Press, Inc.

New York • London • Victoria (AU)
www.HaworthPress.com

Domestic Abuse and the Jewish Community: Perspectives from the First International Conference

Domestic Abuse and the Jewish Community: Perspectives from the First International Conference has been co-published simultaneously as *Journal of Religion & Abuse,* Volume 6, Numbers 3 and 4 2004.

Monographic Separates from the *Journal of Religion & Abuse*™

For additional information on these and other Haworth Press titles, including descriptions, tables of contents, reviews, and prices, use the QuickSearch catalog at http://www.HaworthPress.com.

Domestic Abuse and the Jewish Community: Perspectives from the First International Conference, edited by Rabbi Cindy Enger, and Diane Gardsbane (Vol. 6, No. 3/4, 2004). *Sensitive, practical answers for the problem of domestic abuse in the Jewish community.*

Sexual Abuse in the Catholic Church: Trusting the Clergy?, edited by Marie M. Fortune, MDiv, DHLit, and W. Merle Longwood, PhD (Vol. 5, No. 3, 2003). *"A remarkable achievement . . . Brings together a number of reasoned multidisciplinary voices. . . . Adds much-needed insight and clarity to this challenging problem. Thoughtful and data-driven. . . . Anyone interested in the topic will benefit from reading this book." (Thomas G. Plante, PhD, ABPP, Professor, Psychology Department, Santa Clara University)*

Forgiveness and Abuse: Jewish and Christian Reflections, edited by Marie M. Fortune, MDiv, DHLit, and Joretta L. Marshall, PhD, MDiv, (Vol. 4, No. 4, 2002). *"Profoundly significant. . . . Uncovering both the misconceptions and the possibilities of forgiveness in the context of radical brokenness, this work makes possible the partnership of justice and transformative healing . . ." (Kristen J. Leslie, PhD, Assistant Professor of Pastoral Care and Counseling, Yale University Divinity School)*

Men's Work in Preventing Violence Against Women, edited by James Newton Poling, PhD, and Christie Cozad Neuger (Vol. 4, No. 3, 2002). *Examines the potential for men/women partnerships to work toward an end to domestic violence and sexual abuse.*

Remembering Conquest: Feminist/Womanist Perspectives on Religion, Colonization, and Sexual Violence, edited by Nantawan Boonprasat Lewis, BDiv, ThM, PhD, and Marie M. Fortune, MDiv, DHLit (Vol. 1, No. 2, 1999). *Addresses the issue of sexual violence against Native American, African American, Filipino, and Thai women from feminist/womanist theological perspectives and advocates for change in how some religious groups interpret women.*

Domestic Abuse
and the Jewish Community:
Perspectives
from the First
International Conference

Rabbi Cindy Enger
Diane Gardsbane
Editors

Domestic Abuse and the Jewish Community: Perspectives from the First International Conference has been co-published simultaneously as *Journal of Religion & Abuse,* Volume 6, Numbers 3 and 4 2004.

The Haworth Pastoral Press®
An Imprint of The Haworth Press, Inc.

New York • London • Victoria (AU)
www.HaworthPress.com

Published by

The Haworth Pastoral Press, 10 Alice Street, Binghamton, NY 13904-1580 USA

The Haworth Pastoral Press is an imprint of The Haworth Press, Inc., 10 Alice Street, Binghamton, NY 13904-1580 USA.

Domestic Abuse in the Jewish Community: Perspectives from the First International Conference has been co-published simultaneously as *Journal of Religion & Abuse*, Volume 6, Numbers 3 and 4 2004.

Cover design by Kerry E. Mack

Library of Congress Cataloging-in-Publication Data

Domestic abuse and the Jewish community: perspectives form the first international conference/Cindy Enger, Diane Gardsbane, editors.
    p. cm.
    "Co-published simultaneously as Journal of Religion & Abuse, Volume 6, Numbers 3 and 4 2004."
    Includes bibliographical references and index.
    ISBN-13: 978-0-7890-2969-6 (hc. : alk. paper)
    ISBN-10: 0-7890-2969-3 (hc. : alk. paper)
    ISBN-13: 978-0-7890-2970-6 (pbk. : alk. paper
    ISBN-10: 0-7890-2970-7 (pbk. : alk. paper)
  1. Family violence–Prevention–Congresses. 2. Family violence–Religious aspects–Judaism–Congresses. 5. Women in Judaism–Congresses. I. Enger, Cindy. II. Gardsbane, Diane. III. Journal of Religion & Abuse.
  HV6626.D63 2005
  296.3´8–dc22
                                                                 2005006296

Indexing, Abstracting & Website/Internet Coverage

This section provides you with a list of major indexing & abstracting services and other tools for bibliographic access. That is to say, each service began covering this periodical during the year noted in the right column. Most Websites which are listed below have indicated that they will either post, disseminate, compile, archive, cite or alert their own Website users with research-based content from this work. (This list is as current as the copyright date of this publication.)

(continued)

(continued)

Special Bibliographic Notes related to special journal issues (separates) and indexing/abstracting:

- indexing/abstracting services in this list will also cover material in any "separate" that is co-published simultaneously with Haworth's special thematic journal issue or DocuSerial. Indexing/abstracting usually covers material at the article/chapter level.
- monographic co-editions are intended for either non-subscribers or libraries which intend to purchase a second copy for their circulating collections.
- monographic co-editions are reported to all jobbers/wholesalers/approval plans. The source journal is listed as the "series" to assist the prevention of duplicate purchasing in the same manner utilized for books-in-series.
- to facilitate user/access services all indexing/abstracting services are encouraged to utilize the co-indexing entry note indicated at the bottom of the first page of each article/chapter/contribution.
- this is intended to assist a library user of any reference tool (whether print, electronic, online, or CD-ROM) to locate the monographic version if the library has purchased this version but not a subscription to the source journal.
- individual articles/chapters in any Haworth publication are also available through the Haworth Document Delivery Service (HDDS).

Domestic Abuse
and the Jewish Community:
Perspectives
from the First
International Conference

CONTENTS

HEALING AND WHOLENESS

PROMISING PRACTICES

CREATING CHANGE

BREAKING THE CYCLE

ABOUT THE EDITORS

Rabbi Cindy Enger formerly directed the Jewish Program at Faith Trust Institute (formerly the Center for the Prevention of Sexual and Domestic Violence), an interreligious organization located in Seattle, Washington. She received her rabbinical ordination from Hebrew Union College-Jewish Institute of Religion. Also an attorney, she previously practiced law in Chicago where she represented children and disabled adults. Rabbi Enger is a member of the central Conference of American Rabbis (CCAR) and is the chairperson of it Rabbic Wellness Committee.

Diane Gardsbane is a leader in developing programs to address domestic abuse in the Jewish community. As Director of Programs for Jewish Women International (JWI) from 1998-2002, she shaped the vision for the 1st International Conference on Domestic Abuse in the Jewish community. She is editor of *Embracing Justice: A Resource Guide for Rabbis on Domestic Violence* and *Healing & Wholeness: A Resource Guide on Domestic Abuse in the Jewish Community* (Jewish Women International, 2002), and of Russian/English versions used in Russia and other Commonwealth of Independent States. With over 25 years experience in project design, program development, research, and writing, Ms. Gardsbane now works as an independent consultant with a focus on gender-based issues for organizations including JWI, the Jewish Program of FaithTrust Institute, House of Ruth Maryland, and the Peace Corps.

About the Contributors

Elana Dorfman, MA, was among the founders of the Rape Crisis Center in Jerusalem in 1981, and served as development coordinator for the Haifa Battered Women's Hotline, which runs the National Hotline for the Prevention of Domestic Violence and Children at Risk. She earned a BA in art history and theatre from Tel Aviv University and an MA in theatre from Emerson College.

Jane Frankel is a social worker at Jewish Community Services, a division of the Jewish Helping Hand Society in Johannesburg, South Africa. She is a coordinator of the Shalom Bayit project, which includes counseling, training, and public awareness. Jane is involved in generic counseling, training of volunteers, and community development outreach work. She has a BA (Hons) in social work and a PDM (Post graduate diploma in management), University of the Witwatersrand.

Rabbi Lisa Gelber currently serves as Associate Dean of the Rabbinical School at the Jewish Theological Seminary of America (JTS). Previously a Chaplain Intern at Harborview Medical Center in Seattle, WA, and a Congregational Rabbi at Herzl-Ner Tamid Conservative Congregation in Mercer Island, WA, she is a member of the board of directors of FaithTrust Institute (formerly the Center for the Prevention of Sexual and Domestic Violence). Rabbi Gelber was ordained from JTS in 1996, and received an AB in religion from Amherst College.

Naomi Graetz has lived in Israel since 1967. She teaches English at Ben Gurion University of the Negev and is the author of three books: *S/He Created Them: Feminist Retellings of Biblical Stories* (Professional Press, 1993), a collection of her original midrashim (second edition Gorgias Press, 2003), *Silence is Deadly: Judaism Confronts Wifebeating* (Jason Aronson, 1998) and *Unlocking the Garden: A Feminist Jewish Look at the Bible, Midrash, and God* (Gorgias Press, 2004).

Nadia Kasvin, MA, is Director of the Immigrant Community Services department at Jewish Family Services in Columbus, OH. A refugee from the former Soviet Union, her career has revolved around immigrants as a resettlement professional. Some of the programs for Russian immigrants started under her direction are: Domestic Violence Prevention and Parent-School

Liaison programs, Outreach to Seniors, Immigration Services, Access to Healthcare for Limited English Proficiency Population, Information, and Referral Services, Career Upgrading, and Retention Services, and Interpretation and Translation Services.

Gus B. Kaufman, Jr., PhD, is a Psychologist and social activist, and has worked to end male violence for over 20 years. Dr. Kaufman co-authored *Responding to Domestic Violence* in *Jewish Pastoral Care* and *The Mysterious Disappearance of Battered Women in Family Therapists' Offices* in *Secrets in Families and Family Therapy.* He has trained therapists in the U.S., Europe, and Israel, and created *Stopping Family Violence,* a curriculum for 40,000 prisoners in Georgia. His latest program, *Retreat from Violence,* incorporates nonviolence, trauma work, and beloved community concepts. See: *www.retreatfromviolence.com*

Toby Landesman, LCSW, BCD, is an activist for safety and tranquility in people's relationships. Ms. Landesman was involved with SHALVA (Chicago) for over 10 years, including editing its newsletter, training speakers, and developing creative art exhibits to raise awareness. She is author of *You Are Not Alone: Solace and Inspiration for Domestic Violence Survivors Based on Jewish Wisdom* (FaithTrust Institute, 2004). Ms. Landesman served on the Advisory Committee for the Jewish Program of FaithTrust Institute and was a volunteer for Bitachon (Safety for Jewish Women) in Chicago in 1987. She works extensively with adult trauma survivors in a private practice, including those molested as children.

Mildred Levison, MA, MSc, currently volunteers as Chair of Jewish Women's Aid's board of trustees (UK), the governing body responsible for strategy, management, and financial control, and she takes personal responsibility for line management of the executive director. Ms. Levison has earned several degrees including MS (Human Resource Development) and MA (Public and Social Administration, Diploma Community Work). She was a local government chief housing officer responsible for refuge and temporary accommodation provision for homeless people and victims of domestic violence.

Esti Palant is Director of Bat-Melech Shelter for Religious Battered Women in Jerusalem, Israel. Ms. Palant has developed programs for the treatment and rehabilitation of special population groups. Her motto is: "It doesn't matter how much time a woman and her children spend in the shelter and what their next step is. The important thing is that they gain strength and the ability to cope with their situation." She is a social worker, married, and the mother of five children.

Ada Pliel-Trossman, MSW, has a long history with Israel's Ministry of Labour and Social Affairs: She has been Deputy Director of the Department of Services for Women and Girls, Director of Services for Women and National Supervisor of Services for Women and Girls, Regional Supervisor of Service for Girls in Distress–both in the Haifa and Tel Aviv regions–and a social worker in the Natanya welfare office. Ms. Pliel-Trossman has also been Social Work Supervisor for MSW and BSW students and conducted a course of "Social Work with Women" at the University of Haifa.

Dr. Amy Robbins Ellison is a member of the Board of Trustees of Jewish Women International and The Task Force on Domestic Abuse in the Chicago Jewish Community. Prior to her June, 2000 relocation to Chicago, she was an Assistant Professor of Anesthesiology at the Albert Einstein College of Medicine/Montefiore Medical Center in the Bronx, NY, where she worked for over twenty years. She was also the Director of Cardiac Anesthesia at the Medical Center. In addition, she is an accomplished musical artist who enjoys singing and playing the piano and cello. Dr. Robbins Ellison's personal saga as a survivor of domestic violence has enabled her to speak publicly on the topic on numerous occasions.

Brenda Solarsh, MA, MS, is the Director of Social Services for the Johannesburg Jewish Helping Hand Society, which incorporates Jewish Community Services and a comprehensive range of services. She was the co-founder of the Shalom Bayit project and has a therapeutic and training responsibility within the project. Ms. Solarsh has an MA degree and extensive experience in social services as a counselor, community developer, manager, researcher, and trainer.

Marcia Cohn Spiegel, MA, is co-author of *The Jewish Women's Awareness Guide*, and *Women Speak to God: The Poems and Prayers of Jewish Women*, as well as many articles in books and periodicals. She works with both women and men to create rituals of healing and celebration. She is a founder of the Alcoholism/Drug Action Program of Jewish Family Service, Los Angeles. She served on the Jewish Advisory Committee of Faith Trust Institute since its inception.

Rabbi David E. S. Stein was a 1988-90 member of the Jewish Working Group on Domestic Violence (Philadelphia) when he began to research the material for this article. Now a freelance editor of Jewish books in Redondo Beach (CA), he is the author of *Ketubah Kit for Rabbis: A Reconstructionist Approach,* eBookShuk.com (2003). His last article for *JORA* was *Initiatives to Address Physical Violence by Jewish Husbands, 218 B.C.E.-1400 C.E. (2001).* Email: <ravsulomm@earthling.net>.

Angela Tashayeva, MA, is a refugee from Russia who has been coordinating a Family Violence Prevention Program in the Russian-speaking and general Jewish communities of Columbus, OH, for the past four and one-half years. Her professional background in education as well as her knowledge of psychology and interpersonal skills have led to Russian immigrant victims coming directly to Jewish Family Services and asking for help. Ms. Tashayeva is responsible for community outreach/education and direct services to victims of domestic violence, including court advocacy, case management, and linkage to services.

Judith Usiskin, MA, CQSW, has worked professionally as a youth and community worker, teacher, social worker, and trainer. She has been involved with Jewish Women's Aid in London as a founding volunteer when it became a national organization, as its chair, and as a member of the board of trustees serving as honorary president. Mrs. Usiskin has a BA (admin.) and an MA, diploma social work, CQSW.

Rabbi Dovid Weinberger of Congregation Shaaray Tefila in Lawrence, NY, lectures regularly on *hashkafa* (reflection) and concepts in *halacha*, with emphasis on education, Shabbat rituals, and rituals relating to health. He recently authored *A Hospital Guide for the Jewish Patient,* published by the Orthodox Union. Rabbi Weinberger is the founder of the Five Town Rosh Chodesh program for women, and lectures often for Shalom Task Force, a national organization dealing with spouse abuse in the Jewish community.

Introduction

We are pleased to present this special volume, featuring a sample of
the many presentations by more than 100 speakers at The First International Conference on Domestic Abuse in the Jewish Community–*Pursuing Truth, Justice and Righteousness: A Call to Action*–held July 20-23,
2003 in Baltimore, MD, USA. The conference, sponsored by Jewish
Women International in collaboration with numerous partners, including
the Jewish Program of FaithTrust Institute, was a watershed event for the
Jewish community. The conference brought together more than 500 participants, who represented the diversity of the Jewish community in the
United States, as well as participants from Argentina, Australia, Canada,
Great Britain, Israel, and South Africa.

The title of the conference, *Pursuing Truth, Justice, and Righteousness,* comes from the biblical book of Jeremiah–*"be'emet, b'mishpat
u'vitzdakah*–with truth, justice, and righteousness"–this is the path of return and blessing, healing, and wholeness. (Jeremiah 4:1-2). These words
conclude the Haftarah, the prophetic portion for the week during which the
conference fell. Indeed, the ancient call of the prophet Jeremiah–words of
rebuke but also of possibility and hope–remains the contemporary call with
regard to ending domestic abuse.

A primary goal of the conference was to begin building a *global* Jewish *movement* to address domestic abuse by bringing people together for
the first time to share their stories as survivors, to engage in networking
and, most significantly, to facilitate collaboration among participants. A
fundamental commitment, which steered the conference program, was the
belief that the global Jewish "community," though divided (sometimes bit-
terly) by politics, religious practice, culture, and geography, could create

[Haworth co-indexing entry note]: "Introduction." Enger, Rabbi Cindy, and Diane Gardsbane. Co-published simultaneously in *Journal of Religion & Abuse* (The Haworth Pastoral Press, an imprint of The
Haworth Press, Inc.) Vol. 6, No. 3/4, 2004, pp. 1-3; and: *Domestic Abuse and the Jewish Community: Perspectives from the First International Conference* (ed: Rabbi Cindy Enger, and Diane Gardsbane) The
Haworth Pastoral Press, an imprint of The Haworth Press, Inc., 2004, pp. 1-3. Single or multiple copies of this
article are available for a fee from The Haworth Document Delivery Service [1-800-HAWORTH, 9:00 a.m. -
5:00 p.m. (EST). E-mail address: docdelivery@haworthpress.com].

Available online at http://www.haworthpress.com/web/JORA
Digital Object Identifier: 10.1300/J154v06n03_01

mechanisms to work together based on shared values about what Judaism teaches about the nature of all relationships, and particularly about intimate and familial relationships.

In some ways, domestic abuse has been acknowledged, written about, and wrestled with by Jews for centuries. Various opinions and understandings, for example, can be found in *halakhic* literature. And yet, paradoxically, domestic abuse in the Jewish community has also been denied, minimized, and silenced.

During the past thirty years, however, as victims and survivors–with great strength and courage–have spoken out, Jewish communities throughout the world also have begun to break their silence and address the issue of domestic abuse. In the United States, more than sixty programs now exist to respond to the needs of Jewish victims and survivors of domestic abuse and to provide public awareness and community education. Included are independent agencies, programs within local Jewish Family Services, and those connected to Jewish Federations or other agencies. In Israel, there are thirteen shelter programs, community-based government centers, as well as ten rape crisis centers. In addition, Argentina, Australia, Canada, Mexico, Great Britain, and South Africa are among the other countries where domestic abuse programs operate in order to address the needs of Jewish women.

In this volume, Elana Dorfman's "Ayelet Program: Mentoring Women Leaving the Cycle of Violence," Nadia Kasvin and Angela Tashayeva's "Community Organizing to Address Domestic Violence in Immigrant Population's in the USA" Jane Frankel and Brenda Solarsh's "Domestic Violence in the South African Jewish Community: A Model for Service Delivery," Mildred Levison and Judith Usiskin's "Jewish Women's Aid: Combating Domestic Violence in the UK Community," Tamar Jinjihash's as well as Ada Pliel-Trossman's "Services for Women and Girls in Israel" demonstrate the diversity of programmatic approaches and practices of Jewish communities throughout the world.

Indeed, around the world, Jewish communities have shifted from denial to acceptance about the reality that domestic abuse does affect Jewish families (although some maintain the myth that it doesn't happen in their particular family or synagogue community). We see genuine concern, active programming, and a growing interest in learning how to respond appropriately. At this historic moment of truth-telling and transformation, our goals shift from ending denial and breaking the silence to creating appropriate responses–which assist victims and survivors to be safe, which hold perpetrators of abuse accountable for their actions, and which contribute toward healing and wholeness of those directly and indirectly impacted. In this way, we participate in the process of making abuse in Jewish homes not unthinkable but intolerable.

The articles published in this journal represent a sampling of the subject matters presented at the conference–"Illuminating the Issue," "Healing and Wholeness," "Promising Practices," "Creating Change," and "Breaking the Cycle." Some were presented in workshop sessions and others as plenary and sub-plenary addresses.

The First International Conference on Domestic Abuse represented a significant moment of hope and healing in the life of the Jewish people. The authors in this volume generously have shared their work, energy, commitment, and vision. It is with deep appreciation that we share their work now.

Rabbi Cindy Enger
Diane Gardsbane
Co-Editors

NOTES

The papers in this volume were first presented at The First International Conference on Domestic Abuse in the Jewish Community–*Pursuing Truth, Justice and Righteousness: A Call to Action,* sponsored by Jewish Women International and Partners, held July 20-23, 2003, in Baltimore, MD. The 2nd International Conference on on Domestic Abuse in the Jewish Community–*Pursuing Truth, Justice and Righteousness: A Call to Action,* is also sponsored by Jewish Women International, was held March 20-23, 2005, in Washington, DC. Information about these conferences, and future events, can be found at *www.jwicalltoaction.org.*

Jewish Women International (JWI) is a community of women joining hands, hearts, and minds to promote peace–in families and in communities in the United States, in Israel and around the world. JWI initiatives serve the Jewish and secular communities by creating local, national, and international programming designed to educate, inform, and challenge the thinking about domestic abuse. JWI programs have trained professionals, volunteers, and advocates; built a collaborative global response to domestic abuse; and produced and disseminated a variety of educational publications and resources. Information about these publications and JWI can be found at *www.jewishwomen.org*

To view JWI's award-winning magazine, *Jewish Woman,* go to:

www.jwmag.org.
Jewish Women International
2000 M Street, North West, Suite 720
Washington, DC 20036
1.800.343.2823
www.jewishwomen.org

Pursuing Truth, Justice, and Righteousness: A Call to Action

Rabbi Cindy Enger

SUMMARY. This is one of the Opening Plenary Keynote addresses at The First International Conference on Domestic Abuse in the Jewish Community–*Pursuing Truth, Justice and Righteousness: A Call to Action*, sponsored by Jewish Women International and Partners held in Baltimore, MD. The address was on July 20, 2003, 20 Tammuz, 5763. *[Article copies available for a fee from The Haworth Document Delivery Service: 1-800-HAWORTH. E-mail address: <docdelivery@haworthpress.com> Website: <http://www.HaworthPress.com> © 2004 by The Haworth Press, Inc. All rights reserved.]*

KEYWORDS. Jewish community, domestic violence, mourning, healing, wholeness

I confess that in imagining this moment, in preparing my plenary remarks, I considered asking that we simply sit here–together in silence–allowing the strength and extraordinariness of this moment to fully sink in. Fifteen minutes of silence might move us more than any words.

But then I thought perhaps that wasn't a very good idea. Fifteen minutes and we may become a bit restless. But let's take a moment–to

---

[Haworth co-indexing entry note]: "Pursuing Truth, Justice, and Righteousness: A Call to Action." Enger, Rabbi Cindy. Co-published simultaneously in *Journal of Religion & Abuse* (The Haworth Pastoral Press, an imprint of The Haworth Press, Inc.) Vol. 6, No. 3/4, 2004, pp. 5-10; and: *Domestic Abuse and the Jewish Community: Perspectives from the First International Conference* (ed: Rabbi Cindy Enger, and Diane Gardsbane) The Haworth Pastoral Press, an imprint of The Haworth Press, Inc., 2004, pp. 5-10. Single or multiple copies of this article are available for a fee from The Haworth Document Delivery Service [1-800-HAWORTH, 9:00 a.m. - 5:00 p.m. (EST). E-mail address: docdelivery@haworthpress.com].

Digital Object Identifier: 10.1300/J154v06n03_02

experience each other–faces of hope, faces of courage, faces of love–signs of God's presence, right here, right now, in our midst. Breathe it in. Soak it in.

Out of silence, in the opened space, the song of gratitude is born.[1]

I feel very grateful. It has been a pleasure and a privilege to serve on the planning committee for this First International Conference on Domestic Abuse in the Jewish Community. I thank Lori Weinstein, Millie Sernovitz, Diane Radin, Kathy Morrell, the other members of the planning and advisory committee, and a special thanks to Diane Gardsbane for the opportunity to work with all of you.

And I feel very grateful to be able to link myself to the growing chain of tradition of those working with and within our religious communities to prevent and respond to domestic violence. I want to offer thanks in particular to Rabbi Julie Spitzer (*zichrona livracha*);[2] my colleagues at the Center for the Prevention of Sexual and Domestic Violence, Rev. Marie Fortune, and Rev. Thelma Burgonio-Watson; my colleague working with the Muslim community, Sharifa Alkhateeb; the women and men who serve on the Center's National Jewish Advisory Committee; and my teachers, Rabbi Julie Schwartz and Dr. Jonathan Cohen.

Let's pause for one more moment. Look around. Soak it in.

Individually, organizationally, programmatically, geographically, religiously, we are a diverse group. In the past ten or so years, we have accomplished much to end the silence of shame and denial, to acknowledge that domestic violence exists in the Jewish community, to say that it's not okay, and to implement programs that help us become communities that are safe, where we hold each other accountable and journey together towards healing.

Our work, as we well know, is far from finished. We call each other and the entire Jewish community to action. This is why we have gathered here: because we **can** do better–in our teaching and our text analysis, in our fundraising and our fund decision-making, in our institutional policies, procedures, and programmatic priorities.

We can do better in our synagogues and day schools, in our seminaries and summer camps, in our rabbinical organizations and rabbinic courts, in our community centers and campus Hillels, in our Jewish Family Services and Jewish Federations, in our youth programs and young adult programs, in our brotherhoods and women's organizations–at every level, in every Movement, and in every region.

We can do more to delve deeply into the dynamics of domestic violence, to declare that abuse is a sin, to see that Antisemitism and external oppressors are not the only challenges to Jewish survival. With each instance of domestic violence, Jewish survival is directly threatened–one person, one sacred partnership, one family, one community at a time. If we take seriously Jewish survival, and certainly, we do, then we cannot afford to stand by idly and watch our sister bleed.[3]

Speaking words of rebuke to the people of Israel, the prophet Jeremiah warns of pending destruction, pain and exile. Yet he also proclaims the path of return and repentance: *be'emet, b'mishpat u'vitzdakah–with truth, justice, and righteousness*–then blessing will come (Jeremiah 4:2).

Throughout the world, many of our congregations will read these words from Jeremiah this coming Shabbat. In our annual cycle, we have entered a three-week period of mourning. It began this past Thursday and will conclude with a low point of communal lament on Tisha B'Av, the ninth day of the month of Av, which this year falls on August 7th.

On Tisha B'Av, we mourn the destruction of both Temples in Jerusalem. We recall our many exiles and communal losses. It is a day of fasting and mourning. We read the biblical book of Lamentations, a text of raw pain, which depicts the destruction of Jerusalem in 587 BCE. On Tisha B'Av, from out of the depths of this annual downpoint, we begin the process of reflection and repentance, drawing us near to the High Holy Day season of return and renewal.

On the Jewish calendar, we have entered a time of descent. It seems appropriate that this conference takes place during our annual three week "dark period," at the height of summer, when it is most light outside. Things, as we know, are not always the way that they seem.

Our annual cycle takes us back to a time when destruction is imminent; the Temple *will* burn. And while Tisha B'Av commemorates an ancient trauma, the day and its liturgies of lament bring to life timeless and universal responses to loss. Its texts give voice to devastating pain. Tisha B'Av invites us into that world. It challenges us to feel. And that is the path of healing.

With truth, justice, and righteousness, announces the prophet Jeremiah, then the blessing of healing will come. Justice is truth in action.[4] And righteousness is justice tempered by an open heart. Drawing from a Talmudic teaching on *tzedakah*, righteousness, Rabbi Judith Abrams writes:

Work is hard, but experience makes it easier.

Experience is hard, but compassion may stem from it.

Compassion comes hard, but sadness makes us see the necessity for it.

Sadness is hard, but somehow our hearts bear it.

Having a heart is hard, but the alternative is losing our connection with life and love.

Love is hard, and it fades into memory.

Memory is painful, but forgetting is worse.

Forgetfulness is strong, indeed, but gentle reminders blow the cobwebs away.

Gentle reminders connect us to times past, but over time death comes to us all.

Death is hard and the only salvation from it is to do good deeds, which remain behind us in perpetuity, as it is written, "Tzedakah saves [us] from death." (Proverbs 10:2).[5]

Truth, justice, and righteousness. What is truth? And what do we know to be true?

What's true is that each one of us is created in God's image—precious and unique.

What's true is that by abuse and denial, we've hurt each other deeply.

What's true is that the wounds of our people run deep—but so does the possibility of wholeness.

What's true is that in order to heal, we need to sit with our pain. In the words of Rachel Adler, "We must consent to be bereaved in order to be renewed."[6]

A component of this conference is the development of a communal call to action. We may not think that to sit with pain or to be bereaved has anything to do with action.

But mourning is a process, a journey of effort and action, a process, which calls for courage. One of the tasks of mourning is experiencing and expressing the pain of grief. Experiencing the feelings connected with loss is far from easy. But, as Anne Brener teaches: "The only feelings that do not change are those that are ignored. Only by facing our feelings do we learn and grow. Pain has a size and a shape, a beginning and an end. It takes over only when not allowed its voice."[7]

Part of the point of this conference is to make space that is safe, to create space to voice pain, to be with pain long enough to effect healing–not only here but in our communities when we go home. Each incompleted task of mourning will be remembered until completed.[8] The courage to be with pain is the path of healing. Perhaps it is the only path.

And right now it is calling us to action.

Look around. See our faces. Look around. Breathe it in.

I conclude with a prayer. In the words of my teacher, Marcia Falk:

Let us bless the source of life,
source of the fullness of our knowing.

May we learn with humility and pleasure,
may we teach what we know with love,

and may we honor wisdom
in all its embodiments.[9]

May it be so.

NOTES

1. Marcia Falk, *The Book of Blessings: New Jewish Prayers for Daily Life, the Sabbath, and the New Moon Festival* (Boston: Beacon Press, 1996), p. 241.
2. May her memory be for a blessing.
3. See Leviticus 19:16.
4. Joseph H. Hertz, *Sayings of the Fathers* (New York: Behrman House, Inc., 1945), p. 27 (commentary to Avot 1:18).

5. Rabbi Judith Z. Abrams, PhD, midrash adapted from Babylonian Talmud, Baba Batra 10a.

6. Rachel Adler, *Engendering Judaism: An Inclusive Theology and Ethics* (Philadelphia: The Jewish Publication Society, 1998), p. 170.

7. Anne Brener, *Mourning & Mitzvah* (Woodstock, VT: Jewish Lights Publishing, 1993), p. 4.

8. William Worden, *Grief Counseling & Grief Therapy* (New York: Springer Publishing Company, 1991) (2nd Edition), p. 10.

9. Marcia Falk, *The Book of Blessings,* p.168.

Voice of a Survivor:
Opening Plenary Keynote Address

Amy Robbins Ellison

SUMMARY. Dr. Ellision tells her personal story at the Opening Plenary Session of The First International Conference on Domestic Abuse in the Jewish Community–*Pursuing Truth, Justice and Righteousness: A Call to Action*, sponsored by Jewish Women International and Partners, July, 2003, in Baltimore, MD. *[Article copies available for a fee from The Haworth Document Delivery Service: 1-800-HAWORTH. E-mail address: <docdelivery@haworthpress.com> Website: <http://www.HaworthPress.com> © 2004 by The Haworth Press, Inc. All rights reserved.]*

KEYWORDS. Domestic abuse in Jewish community, survivor's voice

Good afternoon. My name is Amy Robbins Ellison and I don't think that all of my credentials are listed in the program but I can tell them to you quickly:

I skipped kindergarten; I was accepted into an accelerated six-year liberal-arts medical school program at age seventeen; I graduated medical school at age twenty-three; I had post-graduate training in internal medicine, anesthesiology and critical care medicine; I

[Haworth co-indexing entry note]: "Voice of a Survivor: Opening Plenary Keynote Address." Ellison, Amy Robbins. Co-published simultaneously in *Journal of Religion & Abuse* (The Haworth Pastoral Press, an imprint of The Haworth Press, Inc.) Vol. 6, No. 3/4, 2004, pp. 11-17; and: *Domestic Abuse and the Jewish Community: Perspectives from the First International Conference* (ed: Rabbi Cindy Enger, and Diane Gardsbane) The Haworth Pastoral Press, an imprint of The Haworth Press, Inc., 2004, pp. 11-17. Single or multiple copies of this article are available for a fee from The Haworth Document Delivery Service [1-800-HAWORTH, 9:00 a.m. - 5:00 p.m. (EST). E-mail address: docdelivery@haworthpress.com].

Digital Object Identifier: 10.1300/J154v06n03_03

chaired numerous hospital committees including substance abuse
and residency review; I have directed national meetings and have
been an invited speaker at many; I have participated in the research
of new drugs; I was Director of Cardiac Anesthesia at a major
medical center in New York City; I have given anesthesia for
emergency open-heart surgery to a woman who was nine months
pregnant *and* in labor who then delivered a healthy baby girl; I
worked in the operating room with a broken leg in a cast while on
crutches; I was co-principal cellist in a doctor's orchestra in the
Bronx for eighteen years; I am renown for the best chicken soup
and matzo balls east of the Mississippi *and* I was battered for ten
years.

Those are my qualifications for having been invited to be here with
you today. I cannot give you statistics on domestic violence, nor can I
reel off resources with ease, but I can tell you my story. And the stories
have to be told–and heard–and told again. For as uneasy as I sometimes
feel in talking about this–my personal struggle–I know that it is essential to speak about it. All I ask is that you lend me your sympathetic ears.

Nearly eight years ago, on Labor Day weekend of 1995, my family
secret became public. It is not important to recount all the details here
except to say that after an incident in which my husband blackened my
eye, my *mother-in-law* (a righteous person), finally had the courage to
call the police who enabled us, with my daughter, to leave and seek refuge at my friends' home nearby. Although my husbands' family knew
of his abusing and battering me for nearly a decade, it was only after my
father-in-law's sudden death two months earlier that my mother-in-law
could step in with a clearer vision and come to my assistance without
being stopped by her *own* husband. Once enveloped in the arms of my
caring friends, that weekend was spent dealing with my husband's hys-
teria at my having left our home with our daughter, his attempts at
bringing us back home–physically–his attempt to end his life, and multiple conversations with family, friends, and therapists. The police were
involved no fewer than seven times over the course of that three-day
weekend. But the most dramatic moment of that holiday weekend was
not his suicide attempt, was *not* his endless middle of the night phone
calls, or *even* the police officer's concern about my husband's reputation–the *most* dramatic moment of that weekend was that I returned
home.

And then what happened–a verbal agreement was made between the
two of us in my husband's therapist's office and it sounded viable: I

would get an Order of Protection, *he* would attend a batterer's group (again), *his* substance abuse problem would be addressed formally, and he would *never again* raise his hand to me. And then, I began to feel completely isolated. My friends, who were now in the know, were silently distressed at my return home. Invariably, after a short period of calm, during which time *none* of the items in our verbal contract were adhered to, the abusive behavior started again in full force until I asked for help in December of that same year. My friends investigated and found resources for me and linked me up with appropriate counsel and a date in Family Court–a highly imperfect legal arena that in these circumstances, however, can offer some immediate relief. It took eighteen months and over two hundred thousand dollars to extricate myself legally from my marriage, to protect myself (at least on paper), and to limit and structure time spent between my daughter and her father.

But *even* with my newfound freedom of being allowed to watch the eleven o'clock news in bed, or being allowed to sleep after working for twenty-four hours straight having kept patients alive undergoing open-heart, or being allowed to spend time with my friends, my anxiety and fear did not diminish totally. Much of that which he had threatened if ever I was to break-up our marriage had, in fact, come to pass. My friends were stalked, my career and livelihood were placed in jeopardy by letters written by him to various medical licensing and certification bodies, and Orders of Protections were violated on more than one occasion resulting in his incarceration twice.

And why didn't I leave sooner?–for all the reasons that battered women cannot and do not leave: fear of retaliation, a degree of denial, the belief that I could "fix" anything, the harrowing logistics of the break-up of a marriage, living the complicated life of a single parent, and a host of others.

Certainly when I look at my life now and my life then I can hardly make the comparison. I am almost unable to remember the detail, though if pressed, I can conjure up the images of being shoved, choked, doused with water from a spray bottle, stalked throughout my home over the course of a weekend, or going to work and calmly and convincingly explaining away bruises on my back while I changed into operating room garb in the locker room alongside my colleagues. I *never* forget however, the fact that so much of this violence was witnessed by a small child whose *only* concerns should have been who she was going to play with tomorrow, what spelling words she had to know this week, or whether she wanted a peanut butter sandwich or a yogurt in her lunchbox. Instead, she sometimes found herself planted directly between her two parents with courageously outstretched Barbie-like arms, hoping to end the onslaught–or how she repeatedly punched her father's back as he kicked me while I lay curled up on the floor in a corner. Now, my daughter has learned ever so slowly that there are no longer any secrets, that violence is *not* normal or acceptable (even when it comes from someone you love) and that there can be and are serious consequences to our actions. She also knows that our home is very, very calm now–that a person is entitled to privacy (even if that person is a child), and that we speak the truth.

I am convinced it is often difficult, and at times tragic events that can force us to re-evaluate one's life and direction. When I was given my first opportunity to speak in October 1997 at Congregation B'nai Jeshurun in New York City, I felt blessed. And then, in October of 2002, along with six other adults, after completing a year of study, I became a Bat Mitzvah. Our Torah portion was the beginning of Genesis, as the reading of the entire Torah had just been completed on Simchat Torah. As it happens, many of my speaking opportunities have coincided with Domestic Violence Awareness Month, October, *always* on the heels of Shabbat B'reshit (the beginning of Genesis) and the story of humankind's creation–which is for me–my "re-creation." For this reason I have become quite "attached" to that particular time of year. And in this "re-creation" of mine, I have allowed myself to grow and to open my heart for giving and receiving love, to move beyond fear and into strength and to be thankful and appreciate more of life's gifts. My journey took me from New York to Chicago three years ago where I was pulled towards my husband Allan–for whom I had been searching before I even knew that I was on such a quest. He was the beacon that illuminated my path, previously dark and scary. Like Eve was to Adam, he is my *ezer kenegdo*, my helpmate, whose steadfast and unconditional love has guided me to health, wholeness and fulfillment.

We are all here to be vocal; we are here to make some noise, but more importantly, we are here for those who come after us. I am here for my daughter Hillary, the light of my life (an unfortunate witness to events that have made her wise beyond her fifteen years), for whom I have tried to provide over these past several years a return to innocence and to create a safe haven by bringing tranquility to our home, and from whom I draw great strength, joy, and an abundance of love. My daughter has been blessed with the gift of a brilliant intellect and a poet's creativity. She has given me her permission to read one of her poems to you today:

Hillary's Poem

And a smack heard from across the hall

sent a young mind racing

in thought

in definition of family

For what is family to this young mind

but a mother a father and a smack heard

from across the hall?

You say your life is hard

That you know suffering

I don't deny you

But who knows what it's like

in my beaten-up shoes

bought by my beaten-up mother

Did you cower in fear when your blood, your father

denied your mother safe harbor?

When that harbor was not home?

When there was no escape from home?

When shiny badges holding guns inquired from you information

you feared answering because

you were afraid you'd never see him again?

And that confusion after all these years

The utter confusion

of how can you love a man who's capable of terror

of destruction

of pain

of complete turmoil

of the unthinkable?

How do you love a man who kills you every day?

How do you love a man who drags your six-year-old body into traffic to escape the "witch" at the wheel?

How do you love a man who teaches you to fear others?

How do you love a man who enjoyed seeing his woman squirm?

How do you love a man who never saw you for what you were?

How do you love a man of suspicion?

And I do.

I've loved his sickness.

Loved everything he wasn't.

Loved the potential.

But potential is only probable

and probability fails.

And so do I.

I fail to learn.

I fail to learn that the man I love will never change

I fail to learn that the man I love will never see

his daughter, grown and intelligent, choosing the

right path from his mistakes.

If life is based on cause and effect than I am here today

writing in this tear-stained journal

because of the man who I love.

I love what I don't see.

And I've stopped searching.

By permission of author
Hillary Danis, age 15, 2/18/2003

A Shelter for Orthodox
Jewish Women in Israel:
The Experience
of Helping Religious Women
Escape Domestic Abuse

Esti Palant

SUMMARY. This article is based on a presentation made at The First International Conference on Domestic Abuse in the Jewish Community–*Pursuing Truth, Justice and Righteousness: A Call to Action,* sponsored by Jewish Women International and Partners, held in July, 2003, in Baltimore, MD, USA. *[Article copies available for a fee from The Haworth Document Delivery Service: 1-800-HAWORTH. E-mail address: <docdelivery@ haworthpress.com> Website: <http://www.HaworthPress.com> © 2004 by The Haworth Press, Inc. All rights reserved.]*

[Haworth co-indexing entry note]: "A Shelter for Orthodox Jewish Women in Israel: The Experience of Helping Religious Women Escape Domestic Abuse." Palant, Esti. Co-published simultaneously in *Journal of Religion & Abuse* (The Haworth Pastoral Press, an imprint of The Haworth Press, Inc.) Vol. 6, No. 3/4, 2004, pp. 19-29; and: *Domestic Abuse and the Jewish Community: Perspectives from the First International Conference* (ed: Rabbi Cindy Enger, and Diane Gardsbane) The Haworth Pastoral Press, an imprint of The Haworth Press, Inc., 2004, pp. 19-29. Single or multiple copies of this article are available for a fee from The Haworth Document Delivery Service [1-800-HAWORTH, 9:00 a.m. - 5:00 p.m. (EST). E-mail address: docdelivery@haworthpress.com].

KEYWORDS. Domestic abuse, Orthodox Jewish women, Israeli shelters, transitional housing

Abuse is abuse, regardless of culture and religious belief. There is no question that in general, the experience of domestic abuse covers the same gamut in the religious world as it does in the general population. However, in our experience as the only shelter that serves Orthodox Jewish women in Israel, there are some distinct aspects to the experience of the religious Jewish woman suffering domestic abuse.

Bat-Melech is the only one of the 14 domestic abuse shelters in Israel that is designated for religious Jewish women and their children. Like other shelters, Bat-Melech provides these women and children with a safe, supportive, and nurturing refuge from the perpetrators of the abuse, as well as with professional counseling, and emotional and legal support to help them recover from their experiences and regain the strength to rebuild their lives.

This article will address the differences between Bat-Melech, as a shelter for religious women, and other shelters. It will briefly outline the unique difficulties facing religious Jewish women escaping domestic abuse in terms of their decision to come to the shelter, the various treatments they receive in the shelter, and their reintegration into community life upon leaving the shelter. This could be the abstract.

In order to fully understand the unique needs of religious women and thus the services provided by Bat-Melech, it is important to be familiar with the Jewish sources that are relevant to the topic. On one hand, sources dating back to the 12th century that show complete condemnation of any form of violence against women, and on the other hand, sources describing the reverence that Judaism holds for the institute of marriage.

Until the 12th century, the matter of violence between husband and wife was not dealt with in Jewish sources, probably because it was a rare phenomenon. Since then, it has appeared a number of times:

> One who beats his wife should be dealt with more severely that one who beats his friend.[1]

> If a husband physically harmed his wife, the Jewish court has the authority to punish him, excommunicate him, ostracize him, whip him and oppress him with all types of oppression . . . for one must honor her more than himself.[2] (Rabbenu Yerucham)

Rabbenu Peretz (12th century) in his legislative measures was amazed that the community was not shocked and did not respond severely to domestic abuse:

> The sound of the cry of our nation's daughters is heard from a distance regarding Jewish men who raise their arms to beat their wives. Who empowered the husband in this matter to hit his wife? Is he not already admonished against hitting anyone from among Israel?

> We have heard that several women from among Israel cry out in this regard and are not answered in their communities. We have therefore strongly issued a decree and oath binding upon every man among Israel to enter into an oath at the request of his wife or one of her relatives . . . that he does not hit his wife out of anger, in a wicked manner, or in a humiliating manner, for this is not done among Israel. And if, Heaven forbid, there is sprouting a poison weed that will disobey our word by no abiding by this measure, we order the Jewish court of that location that the cries and shouts of her relatives shall reach it, to allocate for her financial support according to her status . . .[3]

Rav Ezra Hadaya, zt"l, a member of the Supreme Rabbinical Court in Israel in the 1930s, rebuked his colleagues for failing to recognize the character of the violent husband and agreeing to give him a "trial period," and for their tendency to blame the wife.

> Who can guarantee that his mouth does not speak falsely? And even if this is done only as a trial for several months, if the trial does not succeed, he will once again be forced to consent to her demands for a divorce. His previous actions render him a lion in ambush after all that he has done in the past. As Rav Yisrael Lifshitz[4] said, "If they were yours, would you do this to them?"[5]

It seems clear from these and other similar sources that violence against women is regarded in Judaism as unforgivable. Jewish law, in fact, rules that the violent husband should be ostracized from the community. Ostracism is considered among the most severe punishments for a religious Jewish man, whose entire way of life is based on his role as a member of the community (praying in a quorum, attending the synagogue for Torah readings and for other religious and lifecycle ceremo-

nies). However, people tend to be more familiar with the many sources
from the Bible, prayers and Talmud that relate to marriage as the most
important value in Judaism.

We learn, for example, "A man who has no wife–is not a person."
Specifically, regarding the biblical verse "male and female did he create
them and he called their name Adam (person)" [6]–Rav Eliezer says that a
man who has no wife is not a person.[7] The curse "with no possessions"[8]
that is mentioned in the Bible is interpreted by Reb Chasdai in the Talmud
as meaning without a wife.[9] In an interpretation of the verse in the Book of
Ruth that states "A woman finds peace in the home of her husband"[10] it is
said that a woman is not content unless she is in her husband's home.

The classic song "A Woman of Valour,"[11] recited every Friday night
in most observant Jewish households, uses the metaphor of a happily
married couple to describe the relationship between G-d and the Jewish
people.

Regarding the person who helps bring peace between a man and his
wife, it is said: "These are the (few) things which man eats the fruits of
in this world and the principal remains for the world to come."[12] In contrast, regarding the couple that decides to divorce, Rav Eliezer says in the
Talmud: "Even the sacrificial alter (in the Temple) cries for the one who divorces his wife."[13]

These sources, and many other similar ones, are encountered by religious Jewish children in their homes and schools throughout their childhood, ensuring that they reach adulthood with a view of marriage as the
pinnacle of happiness and self-realization.

These types of sources have contributed heavily to the myth still upheld in many Orthodox and Ultra-Orthodox communities in Israel that
domestic abuse cannot exist in a religious home. This merely com-
pounds the isolation of the religious woman in an abusive marriage,
who finds herself contemplating alone, in shame and secrecy, the gap
that exists between the dream and the bitter reality of life with a violent
husband.

UNIQUE MANIFESTATIONS OF ABUSE
IN THE "RELIGIOUS COMMUNITY"

In terms of actual abuse, the experiences of religious women are remarkably similar to those of her non-religious counterpart elsewhere in
the world. It is possible, however, to characterize two particularly "reli-

gious" manifestations of abuse that we have seen in the cases of women
who have come to our shelter.

1. Abuse That Relates To Religious Observance

This includes three types of abusive behaviors on the part of the husband that relate to religious observance:

- Forcing his wife to transgress religious commandments. For example, forcing his wife to have sex during her menstrual period, a
  time in which the couple is forbidden to engage in sexual relations
  by Jewish law.
- Being obsessively and needlessly particular about minutiae of religious law. For example making his wife repeatedly check and
  clean vegetables from imaginary insects for hours at a time.
- Using regular religious ceremonies to humiliate and subjugate his
  family. For example, a case where a man would return from synagogue on Friday night and go to sleep, not allowing anyone else to
  eat the Sabbath dinner until the ritual blessings over wine and
  bread had been made. He would then wake up his wife and children at 2 a.m. to conduct the Sabbath meal.

2. The Timeframe of the Abuse Before the Woman Turns to a Shelter

Our experience has shown religious women who are subjected to domestic abuse will wait significantly longer and undergo a greater level
of abuse before coming to a shelter. This is based on informal compari-
sons that have been made between women arriving at Bat-Melech compared with non-religious women who come to other shelters in Israel.
This directly relates to the reluctance on the part of religious women to
break up even an abusive marriage in light of the religious premium
placed on the institute of marriage, as discussed below.

DIFFICULTIES FACED BY RELIGIOUS WOMEN IN COMING TO A SHELTER

The act of coming to a shelter, while not necessarily signaling an
end to the marriage, is nonetheless a public admission that a marriage
has problems. A woman who has been taught all her life that marriage
is of supreme importance, finds it very difficult to take such a step. It is

not unusual to hear a woman who has come to the shelter say, "My mother prefers that I die as a married woman, than live as a divorced woman." The reluctance to break up a marriage, however dysfunctional, explains the many attempts made to reconcile the couple by Rabbis and other counselors who often deal with the woman before she comes to the shelter.

Despite the fact that divorce is a legitimate option in Jewish law, and despite the unequivocal stand against domestic violence taken by the rabbis, an unbroken family unit is still considered preferable. Children of divorced parents, or from families where the husband is abusive, are severely stigmatized, regardless of their personal character. They have difficulty being accepted into good schools, and their chances of marrying "well" are seriously diminished. This increases the ambivalence felt by women suffering abuse, who are torn between their desire to escape the violence, and their confusion over what is best for their children, to stay or to leave. In some cases, a woman, especially one from a very Ultra-Orthodox community, will receive a great deal of support from family and friends while she remains at home. However, once she comes to the shelter, 'washing her dirty laundry in public' as they see it, often even her closest family will turn their backs on her.

In addition, in more than 80% of cases, the catalyst that finally compels a woman to leave her abusive husband is not the abuse she herself suffers, but rather her concern that someone else is being affected by the abuse, usually her children. One woman who came to the shelter told how her abusive husband had insisted that their three children, aged seven, eight, and ten, be in bed when he came home from work. Since he sometimes arrived home as early as 3:30 in the afternoon, she had to have the children already in their beds at that hour, and in order that they shouldn't go without dinner, she would puree all their food so they could drink it through baby bottles. When her children began suffering digestive problems, she realized she had to leave. It is important to realize that throughout this period this woman had simultaneously suffered severe beatings, some that resulted in hospitalizations, yet this did not move her to leave.

THE RELIGIOUS SHELTER VS. OTHER SHELTERS

Despite the enormous difficulties inherent in leaving their husbands and homes and coming to a shelter, some of which are described above, each year tens of women and their children come to Bat-Melech. Unfortunately, tens of others must be turned away due to lack of space.

There are a number of factors that Bat-Melech has to take into account in order to ensure that the shelter enables the women to live a completely religious lifestyle:

1. Jewish Laws

The shelter is strictly kosher and the facilities and services adhere to all the restrictions and laws of the Shabbat, for example, with technical adaptations to emergency equipment such as the video intercom and alarm system. In addition, all the customs and commandments related to the Jewish holidays and the Sabbath are fully observed at the shelter, for example blowing the rams horn on the New Year, and reading the story of Esther on Purim.

2. Treatment and Rehabilitation

In order to ensure greater understanding of the issues and dilemmas facing the women, and to facilitate the development of trust in the shelter staff, all staff members are religiously observant. The staff includes people from all streams of religious Judaism; modern Orthodox, Ultra-Orthodox, Ashkenazi, and Sephardi. This means that despite the many types of religious women who come to the shelter, each can find a staff member who knows and identifies with her particular customs and views.

Bat-Melech actively involves Rabbinical authorities in treatment. Many of the women who come to Bat-Melech have already consulted with Rabbis, and for many of them such a step would not be considered without their Rabbi's approval. The social workers in the shelter encourage this connection, particularly in relation to crucial life decisions, since the involvement of a Rabbi grants legitimacy to the woman in her choice, and when she leaves the shelter, eases her integration back into her community.

An issue that does not arise in other shelters is the need for the woman to choose a legal framework within which to pursue her case. In Israel, there are two parallel legal systems, the Religious and Secular Courts. Divorce is granted only by the Religious Courts, while other procedures such as custody and alimony can be decided by either court. Many in the Ultra-Orthodox community do not grant any legitimacy to the secular legal system since it does not operate according to Jewish law. Bat-Melech recognizes the right of each woman to decide if she wishes to undertake legal proceedings in the Secular Courts in addition to the Religious Courts.

3. The Children in the Shelter

Since larger families are more common in the religious community, the number of children that come to the shelter is on average three times that in other shelters. Sometimes a woman will arrive at the shelter with ten or more children. This results in a need for additional staff in order to provide each child who has experienced or witnessed abuse with individual attention, to ensure that they do not grow up to perpetuate the cycle of abuse.

After a professional assessment of each child's situation and the risks involved in each case, the children are sent daily from the shelter to schools in the community. Unfortunately, because of the stigma attached to broken homes that still exists among sections of the religious community, children from the shelter are often not accepted into some of the better schools, even if they are outstanding students. Bat-Melech makes every effort to send each child to a school that suits his or her religious beliefs in order not to add to the many stresses and difficulties that already affect each child in the shelter.

THE CHALLENGE OF ESTABLISHING AN INDEPENDENT LIFE

Most of the women who leave Bat-Melech (75 percent of the women in 2002) do not return to their husbands, choosing instead to begin an independent life. This is more than three times the number of women from other shelters in Israel. The reason for this is probably the fact that religious women tend to come to the shelter at a very late stage (as mentioned above), having already experienced severe abuse, and having previously tried every other method of resolving the situation beforehand.

The transition to an independent life is difficult for any woman leaving a shelter, but exponentially more so for religious and especially Ultra-Orthodox women. Most of these women have gone straight from living under their parents' authority to their husband's, without ever having lived alone. Independence is extremely threatening to these women, and the knowledge that they belong to a community where divorce is rare, and single women and single mothers hold very low status, makes it even more difficult.

Recognizing the challenges involved in establishing an independent life and the associated difficulties, we invest a lot of thought and time into this aspect of treatment:

1. Choices

We deliberately provide many opportunities for the women to exercise their decision making abilities, with choices of therapy; participation in shelter activities; menu planning; and more. This is designed to lessen the dependence that has been instilled in them through years of abuse.

2. Professional training

We encourage every woman to study a profession that will enable her to support herself and her family, for example book-keeping, computers, or librarianship. The options are varied and depend on her talents, abilities, and emotional strength. Where necessary, Bat-Melech also finances the necessary courses.

3. Transitional apartments

Bat-Melech runs two transitional apartments that enable women to experience a measure of independent living while still receiving support, guidance, and therapy from shelter staff. Over a period of approximately six months in these apartments, the women begin to develop financial independence and continue to use the services of the shelter, including therapy, legal assistance, and children's programs. In this way the women can test their ability to cope with the new situation while still supported in times of need by the shelter staff.

4. Ongoing support of women who have left the shelter

Bat-Melech retains a social worker who is responsible for remaining in contact with women who leave the shelter and helping facilitate their successful integration into the community. She assists them with any difficulty and provides all manner of support, ranging from presents and food for holidays and birthdays, to mediation with the community. She remains in contact with all women who leave the shelter, whether they live independently or return to their husbands.

CONCLUSION

Most of the difficulties faced by an Orthodox woman escaping domestic violence, as well as her treatment in the shelter and the ambivalence that accompanies her leaving the shelter, are very similar to those of any other woman in her situation. However, there are a number of unique obstacles that are directly linked to her religious beliefs, most of them stemming from the supreme value with which Orthodox Judaism views marriage. Despite the extremely negative view taken by Jewish sources of violence against women, and despite the fact that Judaism allows for divorce, the institution of marriage is still seen as being sacred and inviolable. This makes it all the more difficult for a religious woman to take the active step of leaving her marriage–even if it is abusive. Unfortunately, the ramifications of this step on the future of her children are still very significant, even more so in Ultra-Orthodox communities, particularly in the areas of education and future marriage opportunities.

The brave woman who chooses to break the cycle of violence, usually does so because she feels her children are being hurt. At Bat-Melech's shelter she receives therapy and can begin to heal her life in an environment that does not compromise her religious beliefs and practices. This is ensured by the religious staff, participation of rabbis in the treatment, and adherence to Jewish law in all aspects of shelter services. Most of the women who take the bold step to come to the shelter do not end up returning to their husbands, since they generally have tried every other method to resolve the difficulties in the relationship before they come.

Recognizing the unique difficulties faced by religious women in establishing an independent life, we devote special effort to helping the women through this important transition.

It is important to note that given the great power and influence that the religious community holds over its members, it is vitally important to increase awareness of the problem of domestic violence and to provide young couples with education and guidance in developing appropriate methods of dealing with relationship difficulties.

NOTES

1. Rothenberg, Rav Meir. *Responsa*, Vol. 4, Lvov, 1857.
2. Yerucham, Rabbenu. *Sefer Meisharim* 23:5, Constantinople, 1506.
3. Peretz, Rabbenu B.Z. *Responsa*. Venice, 1539.
4. Lifshitz, Rav Yisrael. *Yakhin U'voaz*. Livorno, 1782.

5. Hadaya, Ezra. *Yaskil Avdi*. Supreme Court Publishings, Jerusalem, 1931.
6. Genesis 5:2
7. Talmud, Tractate Yevamot 63
8. Deuteronomy 28:48
9. Talmud, Tractate Nedarim 41
10. Midrash, Ruth Rabba 1:9
11. Book of Proverbs 31:10
12. Talmud, Tractate Shabbat 127
13. Talmud, Tractate Gittin 90

The Battered Woman
in the Jewish Tradition:
See No Evil, Hear No Evil, Speak No Evil

Naomi Graetz

SUMMARY. This article is based on a presentation made at The First International Conference on Domestic Abuse in the Jewish Community–*Pursuing Truth, Justice and Righteousness: A Call to Action,* sponsored by Jewish Women International and Partners, held in July, 2003, in Baltimore, MD, USA. *[Article copies available for a fee from The Haworth Document Delivery Service: 1-800-HAWORTH. E-mail address: <docdelivery@ haworthpress.com> Website: <http://www.HaworthPress.com> © 2004 by The Haworth Press, Inc. All rights reserved.]*

KEYWORDS. Domestic violence, Jewish law, Jewish tradition

    The myth of the kind gentle, Jewish husband has been broken down. The evidence that Jewish wife beating exists is strong. Statistics and headlines assail us with facts. 'One out of six' or 'one out of seven' Israeli women are regularly beaten at home. The estimated minimum figure is 100,000 battered women in Israel (of whom 40,000 end up hospitalized); the maximum number is 200,000 (which includes the

---

[Haworth co-indexing entry note]: "The Battered Woman in the Jewish Tradition: See No Evil, Hear No Evil, Speak No Evil." Graetz, Naomi. Co-published simultaneously in *Journal of Religion & Abuse* (The Haworth Pastoral Press, an imprint of The Haworth Press, Inc.) Vol. 6, No. 3/4, 2004, pp. 31-48; and: *Domestic Abuse and the Jewish Community: Perspectives from the First International Conference* (ed: Rabbi Cindy Enger, and Diane Gardsbane) The Haworth Pastoral Press, an imprint of The Haworth Press, Inc., 2004, pp. 31-48. Single or multiple copies of this article are available for a fee from The Haworth Document Delivery Service [1-800-HAWORTH, 9:00 a.m. - 5:00 p.m. (EST). E-mail address: docdelivery@haworthpress.com].

Digital Object Identifier: 10.1300/J154v06n03_05

Arab population).[1] It is incontrovertible today, something which was not the case in the mid 70s, that Jewish awareness of the problem is on the rise–though not enough. The average Jewish feminist, who may be alert to the existence of the problem in Israel, may not be aware that a similar problem exists on her own turf. Pick up the Denver newspaper, the Boston *Jewish Advocate*, the *New York Times* and you will hear about rabbis' wives who are beaten by their husbands, surgeons' wives who stay in abusive marriages for 12-16 years, kosher shelters and kitchens for Jewish victims of Domestic Violence in New York City and Boston. The numbers being bandied about in the media vary from 19-25%. The conspiracy of silence is breaking, but not fast enough.

HOW IS WIFE-BEATING HANDLED HALAKHICALLY IN ISRAEL?

The law of the state of Israel gives jurisdiction in matters of personal status to Orthodox rabbinical courts. That means that all matters of marriage and divorce are adjudicated according to *halakhah* (Jewish law) and that the judges are all male, Orthodox rabbis. The Israeli rabbinate has in its power to decide whether a man can be ordered to give his wife a *get* (a bill of divorce). The problem outside of Israel is less serious since there is separation of religion and state. Divorce can be obtained through civil and religious law. The Conservative and Reform movements have largely solved the problem of the husband who refuses to give a *get*. But in Israel, there is no civil marriage or divorce, and the problem of the "anchored" wife, the *agunah* (whose number varies from 1,000 to 10,000 depending on whose side you are) is very real and painful. It is also a political problem. The Orthodox rabbinate has a monopoly on providing religious services–competing religious approaches such as the Conservative and Reform movements are not recognized by the State of Israel–and thus rabbis who sit in rabbinical courts have no incentives to interpret *halakhah* in a way that might favor women. Women who have been beaten and raped by their husbands, whose lives are in danger, cannot get out of their marriages and the rabbinate directly conspires to keep them there. It is a commonplace in Israel that rabbinic courts are sympathetic to men; in contrast to civil courts which favor women, but the latter have no jurisdiction in divorce.

How do rabbinic court judges (*dayanim*) in Israel treat the different opinions in *halakhah*, concerning grounds for divorce? Is physical violence by husbands recognized by *halakhah* as a reason to impose a divorce and do the Rabbinic courts of Israel impose divorces in such instances? In 1993, the Chief Rabbi of Haifa, Sha'ar Yashuv Cohen, ordered a man who was a habitual wife-beater and had been imprisoned for this to give his wife a *get*. Although, Cohen claimed that his ruling was a one time ruling for that particular case (*ad personam*), the media justly played up this unprecedented case. The reason for the media hoopla was that according to Jewish law, divorce is effective only if a man, of his free consent, gives his wife the *get*. The act must be performed of his own free will. If he refuses to give the *get*, or is in any way coerced to do so, the result is the same. His wife is unable to be freed and get a Jewish divorce.

The late President of the Israeli Supreme Court, Y. Kahn (1978), wrote that there were four possibilities for the religious courts when a husband or wife comes before it asking for a divorce, the last one being to impose a divorce on the husband (*kefiyat get*). *Kefiyat get*, is the most problematic, because most Israeli *dayyanim* regard enforced divorce as improper and invalid. Thus a woman who remarries on the basis of an invalid divorce is committing adultery and her children are *mamzerim* (bastards), which is a terrible stigma for the children to bear. They are forbidden by *halakhah* to marry any Jew, except another *mamzer*.

The sages of the Mishnah, the first codification of *halakhah* c. 200 C.E., made it easier for women to get divorced which we can see from the following two sources:

> A man born blemished is not compelled to grant a divorce; R. Shimon ben Gamliel says: When does this apply?–when the blemishes are small, but when the blemishes are large he is compelled to grant a divorce . . . the following are the blemishes which compel him to grant a divorce: when he is afflicted with boils; when he suffers from polyphus [the Talmud explains: bad breath]; if he is a collector [according to the Talmud: a collector of dog feces], or a copper worker, or a tanner [all of which are occupations involving stenches], whether these defects existed when they were married, or came into being after their marriage. (Ket. 7:9-10)

> A divorce which is imposed by Jews is valid; if imposed by non-Jews it is invalid. But if the non-Jewish [court] beats him and tells him to comply with the Jewish court, it is a valid divorce decree. (Gittin. 9:8)

In the light of these two quotations from the Mishnah, the Rabbis of the Jerusalem Talmud added the following instance:

> If a husband declares, 'I will neither feed nor provide for my wife," he is compelled to grant her a divorce . . . If bad breath is a justification for such compulsion [as stated in the above mishnah] her **very life** is far more so. (Y. Gitt. 9:9)

Since there is a clear list of criteria which allows for a forced divorce, rabbinic authorities must decide whether the list is an "open" list or a "closed" list. If the list is a closed list, then one can argue that physical violence is not included and one cannot force the husband of the battered woman to give her a *get*. However, if the list is an open list then rabbis can argue that "her very life" means when her life is at stake and that since this applies to the battered wife, the rabbis can force the husband to give her a *get*.

Those sages, past and present, who choose to ignore the distress of battered women, rate the community's interest in family stability and obedience to rabbinic law as being more important than the suffering of the private individual. The Israeli Rabbinic courts tend to rule strictly and to refrain from imposing divorce in cases of husbands who treat their wives violently, unless the case is an exceptional one of life and death. Many Rabbinic judges tend to rule strictly about enforcing a *get* so as not to call into question the husband's power of free consent to a divorce. Their ruling follows the opinions of such *Rishonim* (early sages) as the Rosh and such *Aharonim* (later sages) as the Hatam Sofer, who held that "since there is a significant disagreement amongst the Rabbis, why take sides in the dispute and produce an improperly enforced divorce?"[2] This ruling of Hatam Sofer has produced the tendency in modern rabbinic courts in Israel to always uphold the husband's right of consent, based on indecisiveness–the very opposite of what courts are supposed to do–decide.

HISTORY OF THE PROBLEM

The history of the abused or battered woman in the Jewish tradition is fascinating. By studying it, we can see how Jewish law and the forces behind it developed. In biblical times, we have examples of women who were psychologically abused and an attitude that may have indicated that there was nothing wrong about physically abusing women. In Mishnaic and Talmudic times, there was no reference to battered women as a class. Indeed Judith Wegner's book on the status of women in the Mishnaic period[3] does not even have a footnote on this topic.

One might argue that the "battered woman" as a class is a category that does not exist until modern times. There is the halakhic category of "rebellious wife," who might have as a cause for her rebellion against her husband the fact that he beats her, but her status is determined by her rebellion against him, and not by what he does to her. She is the object, not the subject of the law.

In rabbinic tradition, divorce is not a preferred option, the assumption being that women would prefer to stay in a bad marriage, rather than risk the social ostracism and economic dangers of living outside marriage. Resh Lakish, a first-generation Palestinian Amora (c. 230 C.E.) verbalized this assumption in his well known saying "A woman would always rather live with a husband than live alone" (*b Kid* 41a).

Women were socialized into staying in a bad marriage because the institutions of marriage and family were considered to be supreme. Divorce was the last recourse. Despite this fact, there is evidence that until the twelfth century, rabbinic attitudes towards the woman who was unhappy in her marriage were fairly lenient. The list of grounds for forced divorce was expanded to include not only an abusive husband, but also one who was distasteful to the wife.

According to Shlomo Riskin, this all changed when Rabbenu Tam insisted "that there was no Talmudic precedent for coercing a husband to divorce his wife on the basis of her subjective claim that he was repulsive to her . . ."[4] Unfortunately, even though Maimonides, another great authority, permitted these grounds, R. Tam's dictum prevails today and a battered woman "who finds her husband distasteful has no legal recourse" to a forced divorce.

Most rabbinic authorities throughout the ages have not upheld the husband's "right" to beat his wife, despite the existence of several prominent sages who are on record as authorizing wife-beating if she deserves it. However, among these authorities, only a few exceptional rabbis were willing to use wife-beating as grounds for forcing the husband to give his wife a *get*.

ATTITUDES IN JEWISH TRADITION TOWARD WIFE-BEATING

The roots of attitudes toward wife-beating lie in Jewish tradition. In order to understand and change attitudes, it is necessary to know from whence they come. Biblical and rabbinic sources which perpetuate bias against women and justify treating women as second-class citizens continue to be studied. These texts form the background for many modern day attitudes toward women. If we wish to improve our society and eradicate such bias, it is important to recognize the problematic nature of these sources as a first step in fighting back.

A useful source to study wife-beating is responsa literature which starts in gaonic times (700-900 C.E.) and continues to be written today. Rabbinic attitudes to wife beating as seen in the responsa can be categorized as follows: Acceptance, Denial, Apologetics, Rejection, and Evasion of Responsibility.

Acceptance

It is somewhat frightening that in recent times, patriarchy is being idealized by some contemporary Jewish women who are choosing a fundamentalist way of life in order to gain security in a world of conflict and ambiguity.[5] The price for this security is an increase in male dominance and the abdication of women's rights as individuals. In the 70s, Lenore Walker called this "learned helplessness" and showed how the process of victimization resulted in psychological paralysis which trapped the woman in the relationship.[6] In the 80s, Jane Jacobs described the process of abdication in terms of "emotional economy." The female develops emotional commitment which is expressed through submission to the male. In return she gets love and emotional support. The reason this happens is that women are socialized to get self-validation through male approval.[7]

Perhaps the worst consequence of this fundamentalist status quo is that it includes acceptance of wife-beating as natural. The view is often expressed that it is man's nature to be aggressive and woman's nature to suffer—and maybe she deserves it.

In this world-view, beating is regarded as a means to an end. Battering can be justified—on occasion, for it is a mitzvah to chastise one's wife for educational purposes. Battering might even be seen as a means to obtaining *shalom bayit*, domestic harmony. The communal unit is perceived to be more important than the individual. There have been many examples of acceptance of wife-beating in the Jewish community throughout the ages.

We find the first such examples among the Babylonian *gaonim* who flourished from the 7-9th century. Rabbi Yehudai Gaon (an 8th century scholar to whom are attributed many anonymous gaonic opinions) writes that:

> A wife's duty is to honor her husband, raise her children, and feed her husband (even from her own hand). She has to wash, cook, grind in accord with what the rabbis have decreed. And when her husband enters the house, she must rise and cannot sit down until he sits, and she should never raise her voice against her husband. Even if he hits her she has to remain silent, because that is how chaste women behave.[8]

R. Shmuel Hanagid (936-1056), a Jewish Courtier, intellectual, and military leader who wrote poetry among other things, advises the husband to beat his dominating wife to put her in her place.

> Hit your wife without hesitation; if she attempts to dominate you like a man and raises her head [too high]. Don't my son, don't you be your wife's wife, while your wife will be her husband's husband.[9]

Although Maimonides says, a man should honor his wife more than his body and love her as his body,[10] and rules that a "Woman is not a captive and should be granted a divorce if her husband is not pleasing to her,"[11] he recommends elsewhere in his codes, the Mishneh Torah, that beating a bad wife is an acceptable form of discipline:

> A wife who refuses to perform any kind of work that she is obligated to do, may be compelled to perform it, even by scourging her with a rod.[12]

What is required work? It is generally understood to mean housework.[13] If she refuses to do this work, then she "may be compelled." What does compel mean? Who compels her? According to the *peshat*, the simplest meaning of the text, it is possible to understand that it is the husband. But one can allow that it is the Jewish court (the *beit din*) as well. Most commentators on this passage, understood it to mean her husband.

Denial

Denial is a form of lying and very often everyone has to cooperate in order to maintain the lie. The person who denies that a problem exists does not have to deal with it. The following examples excerpted from responsa illustrate the attitude of denial:

Abraham Ben David of Posquieres (Rabad, 12-13th century), in his commentary on the Rambam's Mishneh Torah, expressed great surprise at Rambam's ruling that a man may beat his wife and rejected it altogether. "I have never heard of women being scourged with a rod,"[14] he declares. Rabad said this to set standards for Jews who lived in Christian Europe where it was acceptable practice to "educate" women in this way.

Another expression, still heard today, is that it is the "way of the gentiles" to beat their wives, and unseemly for Jews to engage in acts of that sort.[15] Most recently I have heard this comment whenever I tell people the topic of my research. "Isn't Jewish wife-beating an oxymoron?" they ask.

And then there is Rabbenu Tam, the French tosafist (12th century), who said that "wife-beating is unheard of among the children of Israel."[16]

Apologetics

"Apologetics" in Judaism is defined as "that literature which endeavors to defend Jews, their religion, and their culture in reply to adverse criticism."[17] Apologetics was prevalent whenever Jews felt threatened by the surrounding culture. It was used consciously as a tool by Jewish historians of the late nineteenth and early twentieth century. Today, perhaps it is a form of unconscious denial.

The defense of apologetics is connected with anti-Semitism. Jews perceived the world as hostile (and it is naive to think otherwise) so they wanted to look good–both to themselves and to others in order to guard against outside hostility. Apologetics as a defense minimized negative elements in Judaism. Those who used it assumed that Judaism was too fragile to admit to wrongdoing. But Judaism is not a fragile institution. Questioning certain aspects of Judaism does not constitute a threat to the integrity of Judaism. Judaism is not and has never been a monolithic institution; it thrives on controversy and multiplicity of opinions. Unfortunately apology, which starts out by whitewashing, ends up obfuscating the roots of abuse and in the end perpetuates it.

Another danger of apologetics is that it stifles self-criticism. According to Judith Plaskow,

> . . . [C]riticism is an ongoing and essential part of the Jewish feminist project. Not only is criticism a precondition for imaging a transformed Judaism, without a clear critique of Judaism that pre-

cedes and accompanies reconstruction, the process of reconstruction easily can be misconstrued as a form of apologetics.[18]

Worse perhaps is that Judaism is denigrated by the explanations and rationalizations made in order to "guard the law from humiliation."[19] The net result of apologetics is that modern people whose frame of reference is western modernity and who do not accept the halakhic system are lead to question the validity of halakhic analysis for themselves.

How do apologists for Judaism and Jews relate to the problem of wife-beating? Their first reaction is usually to **deny** its existence: Jews don't do it. If they are forced to see that wife-beating is a phenomenon they cannot ignore, they then **marginalize** and state that those Jews who do engage in wife-beating do so less frequently and less violently than do non-Jewish batterers. They will try to **justify** it by claiming that those Jews who actually engage in such behavior don't really hurt their wives, and if they do, perhaps it's for a good reason. Finally, they will **displace** the blame, by shifting it to others: It is not our fault; if Jewish men batter, it is only because of environmental influences.

But apologists rarely get this far. Not only do they rely heavily on denial, they usually **romanticize** Judaism, by depicting a rosy picture of the traditional Jewish family. Jews often quote from those apologists who perpetuate the myth of the happy Jewish family in order to reconfirm their own positive self-image.

Perhaps the classic example of apologetics is that which is found in the Torah edition used in many Orthodox and Conservative synagogues, edited by Rabbi J. H. Hertz (early twentieth century) of England. He compared the status of Jewish women with Christian women. He used wife-beating as his litmus test.

> The respect and reverence which womanhood enjoyed in Judaism are not limited to noble and beautiful sayings. That respect and reverence were translated into life . . . [O]ne test alone is sufficient to show the abyss in actual life, between Jewish and non-Jewish chivalry down to modern times. That test is wife-beating.[20]

Hertz quotes two British historians, J. Coulton and G.M. Trevelyan to show that among non-Jews chastising one's wife by beating her was not only customary but was even formally granted by the Canon Law. In Trevelyan's words: "wife-beating was a recognized right of man, and was practiced without shame by high as well as low."[21] But not by Jews! Christian men beat their wives, Jewish men don't.

He quotes Rabbenu Tam, to show that "This is a thing not done in Israel" and the Shulhan Aruch which "prescribe it as the Beth Din's duty to punish a wife-beater, to excommunicate him, and–if this be of no avail–to compel him to divorce his wife with all the rights she is entitled to in her *ketubah*, her wedding contract (Eben Ha-ezer, CLIV, 3)."

If we compare Hertz's selective quotation from the Shulhan Aruch with the original text we will see that Hertz refers only to those rabbis in the Shulhan Aruch who consider wife-beating grounds for divorce, while ignoring the majority who do not! A major distortion upon which an apologetic stance is based is that the Jewish tradition is monolithic.

Rejection[22]

Rejection is an uncompromising attitude; it looks injustice in the eye; in order to "fix" the state of injustice, and it rejects the status quo which is the root of the injustice. Thus it is a radical approach to life.

The stance of rejection first of all confronts the problem of wife-beating; it neither denies the fact or accepts it nor makes excuses for it. The stance of rejection clearly states that wife-beating is wrong and demands some kind of redress or release of suffering for the victim. Unconditional rejection is the approach of those rabbis who face up to the fact that there is a problem and condemn it thoroughly. The best of them relate to *halakhah* creatively by use of *takkanot* or creative legislation to change the world when they perceive immorality around them.

Most of these responsa date from the 12th and 13th centuries among the Jews of Askenaz in Germany and France. Here we have a clear attitude that rejects the beating of wives without any qualifications. The three most notable examples of rabbis who represent this attitude are Simcha b. Samuel of Speyer, Rabbi Meir of Rothenberg, and R. Perez b. Elijah of Corbeil.

These three European rabbis were very severe with wife batterers. Their severity can be seen in the manner of punishment and in their refusal to allow husbands to force their wives to do their required housework or to beat them for "their own good." These rabbis considered battering as grounds for forcing a man to give a *get*.

Simcha b. Samuel of Speyer, a leading member of the Rabbinical Synod of the Rhine Provinces held in 1223, declared

> It is an accepted view that we have to treat a man who beats his wife more severely than we treat a man who beats a fellowman . . . And a man who does this should be put under a ban and excom-

municated and flogged and punished with various forms of tor-
ment; one could even cut off his hand if he is accustomed to it
[wife-beating]. And if he wants to divorce her let him divorce her
and give her the *ketubah* payment. You should impose peace between them and if the husband does not fulfill his part in maintaining the peace, but rather continues to beat her and denigrate
her, let him be excommunicated and let him be forced by Gentile
authorities to give her a *get* . . .[23]

He stresses her status as wife rather than simply as another individual. His argument is she was given for living, not for suffering. R.
Simcha is one of the few authorities who authorized a compelled divorce as a sanction. It would seem that R. Simcha is relying on the
Mishnah (Gittin 9:8) that accepts a coerced divorce as valid.
     During the 13th century, cases of maltreatment of wives by hus-
bands that came before the Ashkenazi rabbis were treated harshly.
During this time period a *takkanah* was proposed that actually dealt
with the subject of wife-beating. A *takkanah* is a halakhic amendment that changes an existing law. It usually redresses an existing social problem. Not much is known about the *takkanah* of R. Perez b.
Elijah of Corbeil which was reproduced by Louis Finkelstein in his
book *Jewish Self-Government in the Middle Ages*. The subject is wife
beating and we do not know whether it was approved.

The cry of the daughters of our people has been heard concerning
the sons of Israel who raise their hands to strike their wives. Yet
who has given a husband the authority to beat his wife? Is he not
rather forbidden to strike any person in Israel? Moreover R.
I(saac) has written in a responsum that he has it on the authority
of three great Sages, namely R. Samuel, R. Jacob Tam, and R.
I(saac), the sons of R. Meir, that one who beats his wife is in the
same category as one who beats a stranger. Nevertheless we have
heard of cases where Jewish women complained regarding their
treatment before the Communities and no action was taken on
their behalf.

We have therefore decreed that any Jew may be compelled on application of his wife or one of her near relatives to undertake by a
herem not to beat his wife in anger or cruelty or so as to disgrace
her, for that is against Jewish practice.

If anyone will stubbornly refuse to obey our words, the Court of the place to which the wife or her relatives will bring complaint, shall assign her maintenance according to her station and according to the custom of the place where she dwells. They shall fix her alimony as though her husband were away on a distant journey.

If they, our masters, the great sages of the land agree to this ordinance it shall be established.[24]

The *takkanah* of R. Perez b. Elijah of Corbeil was unusually liberal. To allow the wife of a husband guilty of beating her to get alimony from her husband's property and to live separately from him without divorce was a revolutionary measure. Perhaps that is why the *takkanah* failed to gain the support of his colleagues.

Evasiveness

The fifth attitude, **evasion of responsibility,** can also be referred to as the "wringing hands syndrome." On the one hand, rabbis acknowledge that wife-beating is wrong, yet they do not take action to get the woman out of the bad marriage. They evade responsibility for doing anything about it. It is a very complicated attitude and the authorities who respond to questions about wife-beaters often go through tortuous reasoning—which seems illogical and contradictory.

If we look at two responsa of Radbaz (R. David B. Solomon Ibn Avi Zimra), one of the pillars of Jewish life in Egypt and in Palestine during the latter part of the 15th and 16th century, we can see an example of this attitude. Radbaz is sometimes referred to as Me-or Ha-Golah, the Light of the Exile.[25] He strongly objected to the ruling by R. Simcha of Speyer who allowed civil authorities to force a man to divorce his wife, ignoring in the process the mishnah in Gittin on which R. Simcha based his ruling.

We already know that the man who beats his wife transgresses the commandment not to beat to excess, etc. We know that he has the right to rebuke and beat her if she behaves improperly, according to our Torah, in order to bring her back to the right path, for she is under his jurisdiction. However, he is not allowed to beat her for matters which pertain to him personally, for she is not his servant. And even for those improper things (referred to above) there should be witnesses to the deed (otherwise he should not beat her). And if he habitually beats her, he should be punished. There is one who exaggerated in his teaching [this is a clear reference to R. Simcha] and said that we can force him to divorce her, even by use of non-Jews . . .[26]

In a second responsa, Radbaz is more explicit in his opposition to R. Simcha. He refers directly to his responsa and says that "he is surprised that R. Simcha decreed as he did, since if he allows a forced divorce, the children, who would be the issue of a possible re-marriage would be considered illegitimate issue (*mamzerim*)."[27] Thus a woman whose divorce decree is invalid and who then re-marries illegally is committing adultery and causes her children to be considered *mamzerim*. However, a man who re-marries, despite the fact that his wife refuses to accept the divorce decree, might be considered to be behaving improperly, but his children by his second wife are legitimate issue because by biblical law a man is permitted many wives.

We have a double standard which is accepted by all those who are interested in being halakhic Jews, namely that adultery only applies to a married woman. The woman is made to solely bear the responsibility for passing on the stigma of *mamzerut* to her children. Although the rights of women in family law have increased since biblical times—and a woman may not be divorced against her will—she still remains dependent on her husband's willingness to give her a *get*, a writ of divorce. Only the man can grant divorce by his "will." These two examples of the double standard put the woman at the man's mercy, for if he refuses to divorce her there is not much she can do and the threat of stigmatizing children from another man is daunting.

In his responsa, Radbaz refers to another responsa by Rashba (R. Solomon, B. Abraham Aderet) (1235-1310), who lived in Barcelona and was one of the most important writers of responsa:

> A question was asked of him: What is the ruling for a husband who regularly beats his wife, so that she has to leave his home and return to her father's home? The answer is: The husband should not beat his wife. She was given to him for life, not for sorrow. He should honor her more than his own body. The beit din investigates to find who is responsible. If he beats her, she is allowed to run away, for a person does not have to live with a snake. But if she curses him for no reason, the law is with him, for the woman who curses her husband leaves without her ketubah. At any rate I don't

see that the beit din can do more than tell him in strong words not to beat her and warn him that if he beats her, not according to law, he will have to divorce her and give her ketubah.[28]

Although these rabbis accept the notion that there are occasions when a beating might be justified, most of them agree that habitual wife-beating is wrong. But though the wife-beater's action is wrong, the husband cannot be forced to divorce his wife. If there is even a hint of coercion the get runs the risk of being considered invalid.

What underlies the evasive attitude? First is the paramount importance of the sacred institution of marriage in Judaism. The preservation of this institution, one of the linchpins of Judaism (together perhaps with the Sabbath and laws of Kashrut) is more important than a solution to the problem of an individual wife's suffering. For this reason, battering by itself is not sufficient grounds for forcing a divorce. Second, the person who has an evasive attitude accepts the primacy of the male in Judaism as a given, which is reflected in the acceptance of the inviolate nature of the rule that only a man can give his wife a get. Thus with the assistance of rabbinical courts whose attitude is one of evasion, the power of the recalcitrant husband reigns supreme and he can keep his wife under control in an abusive marriage or coerce her to give him blackmail type payments if she wants out.

SUGGESTIONS FOR SOLUTIONS

We have seen that Jewish law gives the authority to the beit din to force a man to give his wife a divorce, but that modern Israeli rabbinic courts do not utilize the authority they possess. Moreover, the procedures in rabbinical courts favor men. Lawyers for women in rabbinical courts cynically recommend to women they defend that they should give the husband what he wants (the car, the house, money, visitation rights, etc.) in order to be granted a *get*. The situation is so bad that a broad-based coalition was formed in order to put pressure on the rabbinate. This group, the international coalition for *agunah* rights, ICAR, suggests the following major proposals:

(1) To **force a get** upon refractory husbands when there are halachic grounds for doing so, as well as to expand the list of causes so as to adapt them to new situations . . .

(2) To recommend to couples about to be married that they sign **pre-nuptial agreements** which would prevent, or at least limit, the phenomenon of *agunot* or women refused divorce. Agreements such as these have been proposed by great rabbis and there is no reason not to use them today.

(3) To use the solution of the **annulment of marriage** by rabbinic court when the husband's actions are improper. This solution was used by Jewish communities in the past and its application should be reintroduced.

(4) To give the *dayyanim* the authority to invoke **civil sanctions** against a refractory husband, such as revoking a driving license, forbidding him to leave the country, blocking his use of credit cards, etc.

(5) To prohibit receipt of recompense for granting a divorce, and to make possible lawsuits on the grounds of extortion against the party demanding such payment. This condition would **prevent the blackmail** which in many instances is associated with the refusal to grant a divorce.[29]

ICAR is an organization that is trying to work within the frame of the religious establishment and which sees itself as committed to an Orthodox interpretation of *halakhah*. Thus its effectiveness as a pressure group is limited because it ignores the halakhic solutions which the Conservative and Reform movements have already proposed. It does not have on its list the need for a *takkanah*, a halakhic amendment which could immediately solve the problems of the *agunot* and redress the basic inequality of women in personal status and law. It does not recognize that the Conservative movement has already annulled marriages and has included pre-nuptial agreements in the *ketubah* since the 1960s (the famous Lieberman *ketubah*).

It is unwilling to threaten the religious establishment with recognition of non-Orthodox groups, so that there will be no monopoly on religion in the State of Israel. When there are competing systems, the rabbinate will have to listen or go out of business. As has been shown, there are many halakhic alternatives available, but there is no incentive (read threat) for the rabbinate to use them. If one thinks about it, it is incredible that present day *halakhah* has managed to ignore the mishnah on *gittin* and the responsa of such rabbis as R. Simcha who based his opinions on that mishnah.

CONCLUSION

What this means for the modern person, particularly the *agunah* (the woman chained to an absent spouse or one who refuses to give her a divorce) in the modern State of Israel, is that there is no halakhic recourse as understood by the Orthodox establishment (OE). Although alternative religious solutions are being suggested by the Conservative and Reform Movements, since they are not recognized by Israeli law, they are not competitive enough as yet to be threatening to the OE.

Unlike Riskin, who takes a rather paternalistic attitude, ("it is up to the contemporary halakhic community to grant the woman her proper due"), one can argue that the halakhic stance *a priori* is inimical towards women.

Women cannot initiate divorce, they depend on their husband's will to get divorced, and they bear sole responsibility for the stigma of *mamzerut*. Until recently, women were not rabbis, and did not have access to learning and thus could not be part of the halakhic process. As of now, only in the Conservative and Reform movements are women ordained as rabbis. The *halakhah* is androcentric, it assumes that women is the "other," it plays down women's roles.[30] Until women are full fledged rabbis in all three movements and all disabilities against women are erased–not because men want to 'grant' women what is her due, but because women are equal to men and it is just and correct to do so–the best course for women is to simply ignore the rulings of those rabbis who discriminate against them and turn to those rabbis who are willing to use the halakhic tools of coercion of marriage (*keffiyat get*), annulment (*hafkaat kidushim*), and prenuptial arrangements (*kidushim al tenai*).

There is a mockery of justice in the Israeli rabbinical court system. The courts cynically argue that women in the State of Israel are finding themselves in more difficult straits than Jewish women in the past because rabbis are unable to impose legal sanctions upon community members and to impose punishments when a member of the community behaves in an unacceptable fashion. Rather than accept the blame, they argue it is the fault of civil legislators who have not authorized rabbinic judges to impose sanctions upon violent husbands or upon husbands who refuse to divorce their wives. However, to give more authority to the same rabbinic courts which have been indifferent to the plight of women is not a viable solution. It is simply a device to shift blame from the rabbinic courts to the secular courts. One might counter instead that we should abolish the rabbinic courts in light of their previous and present record of miscarriage of justice. The people in charge of the functioning of Rabbinic courts in Israel have proven themselves to be neither capable of self-criticism nor of self-reform. The history of today's rabbinical court system is anything but proud and the main sufferers of this arrogance are women.

NOTES

1. Sasha Sadan, "Day of Protest Decries Violence against Women," *Jerusalem Post*, November 26, 1993 (A3).

2. Mordecai Frishtik, "Physical and Sexual Violence by Husbands as a Reason for Imposing a Divorce in Jewish Law," *The Jewish Law Annual*, IX: 168.

3. *Chattel or Person* (Oxford University Press: New York, 1988).

4. *Women and Jewish Divorce*, Ktav Publishing: Hoboken, NJ, 1989, p. xiii.

5. Jane L. Jacobs, "Gender and Power in New Religious Movements," *Religion* 21, 1991:347.

6. Lenore Walker, "Battered Women and Learned Helplessness," *Victimology*, 2, 3-4 (1977-8): 525-534.

7. Jane Jacobs, "The Economy of Love in Religious Commitment," *Journal for the Scientific Study of Religion*, 1984, 23 (2): 166. She quotes Anne Schaef, Women's Reality, Minneapolis, Winston Press, 1981.

8. Otzer Ha-geonim Le-ketubot. pp. 169-70.

9. R. Shmuel Hanaggid, *Ben Mishlei* (edition of S. Abramson (Tel Aviv, 1948), 117, sec. 419.

10. hilchot Ishut, 15: halacha 19.

11. Mishneh Torah, halacha chovel oo-mazik 4, 16.

12. Isshut 21.10

13. In Halacha 3 there is a list of required duties (rochetzet . . . mozeget) See Halacha 5 and 7 as well.

14. As quoted by Isaac Klein, "Introduction," to The Book of Women: Code of Maimonides, Yale Judaica Series, Book IV, Yale University Press, 1972: xxxv-xxxvi.

15. Even haEzer #297.

16. Klein, xxxv-xxxvi.

17. *Encyclopedia Judaica*, vol. 3, 188-20. In the context of Christianity "its function is both to fortify the believer against his personal doubts and to remove the intellectual stumbling blocks that inhibit the conversion of unbelievers." (Encyclopedia Britannica, 486)

18. Judith Plaskow, *Standing Again at Sinai*, Harper and Row: San Francisco, 1990, p. 2.

19. Chaim Seidler-Feller, "Female Rabbis, Male Fears," *Judaism*, 1984:33, p. 81.

20. Rabbi J. H. Hertz of England, his commentary on the Book of Deuteronomy, *The Pentateuch and Haftorahs*, London, 1938 p. 935.

21. Ibid.

22. This section is an abridged form of a forthcoming article in *Gender and Judaism*, T. Rudavsky, editor, NYU Press, 1995.

23. As cited by Joseph Karo, in Bet Yosef, his commentary on the Tur of Yakov ben Asher Even Ha-Ezer 154:1.

24. Finkelstein's translation, p. 217

25. Israel M. Goldman, The Life and Times of Rabbi David Ibn Abi Zimra, Jewish Theological Seminary of America, New York, 1970:1.

26. Responsa project of Bar Ilan, Radbaz responsa, part 3, 447.

27. Responsa project of Bar Ilan, part 4, 157

28. Bar Ilan Responsa Project, Rashba's Responsa, part 7, #477

29. "ICAR's Main Proposals," *Shackled Women,* a pamphlet distributed by ICAR p.o.b. 3171, Jerusalem 91031.

30. cf. Judith Plaskow, "Halakha as a Feminist Issue," *The Melton Journal,* Fall, 1987, pp. 3-5;25.

Did Maimonides Really Say That?
The Widespread Claim that He Condoned Wife-Battering May Be Mistaken

Rabbi David E. S. Stein

SUMMARY. That the famous Rabbi Moses Maimonides (Egypt, 1178) condoned–or even recommended–spousal abuse has been widely reported. The present article finds that this standard, literal interpretation of the passage (*Ishut* § 21.10a) has little to support it. That reading ignores the text's figures of speech. And it fits neither the dynamics of the case, the legal history of the issue, nor the literary context. Rebutting the published "proof" that medieval legal experts read the passage literally, this article suggests that Maimonides' words may have implicitly taken a stand *against* spousal abuse. It concludes by pondering the meaning of the standard view's popularity. *[Article copies available for a fee from The Haworth Document Delivery Service: 1-800-HAWORTH. E-mail address: <docdelivery @haworthpress.com> Website: <http://www.HaworthPress.com> © 2004 by The Haworth Press, Inc. All rights reserved.]*

KEYWORDS. Mishnei Torah, domestic relations, marriage, violence prevention, domestic violence, wife-beating

---

[Haworth co-indexing entry note]: "Did Maimonides Really Say That? *The Widespread Claim that He Condoned Wife-Battering May Be Mistaken.*" Stein, Rabbi David E. S. Co-published simultaneously in *Journal of Religion & Abuse* (The Haworth Pastoral Press, an imprint of The Haworth Press, Inc.) Vol. 6, No. 3/4, 2004, pp. 49-74; and: *Domestic Abuse and the Jewish Community: Perspectives from the First International Conference* (ed: Rabbi Cindy Enger, and Diane Gardsbane) The Haworth Pastoral Press, an imprint of The Haworth Press, Inc., 2004, pp. 49-74. Single or multiple copies of this article are available for a fee from The Haworth Document Delivery Service [1-800-HAWORTH, 9:00 a.m. - 5:00 p.m. (EST). E-mail address: docdelivery@haworthpress.com].

Digital Object Identifier: 10.1300/J154v06n03_06

INTRODUCTION

Those who wish to gauge the historical place of spousal abuse in Jewish life surely pay attention when scholars say that Rabbi Moses Maimonides (1135-1204) "recommended" that husbands beat their wives under certain circumstances.[1] For Maimonides is one of the leading figures in Jewish law, having (among many other achievements) edited a renowned compilation, the *Mishnei Torah*. Completed 826 years ago in Hebrew, every serious student of Jewish lore must reckon with it, for it was accepted as an authoritative legal manual in many Jewish communities for centuries, and among some Jews to this day.[2]

That Maimonides condoned–or even recommended–spousal abuse is widely stated in contemporary literature, especially in English. It appears in more than twenty journals, books, and reference works addressing a wide range of topics.[3] The authors concerned are reputable scholars with impressive credentials–including prominent historians, famous rabbis, and well-regarded writers on women's studies and on domestic violence.

All of these authors are referring to a terse sentence–fifteen words long–that comprises the first portion of the tenth entry in the twenty-first chapter of the *Mishnei Torah's* section on domestic relations (*Ishut* § 21.10a). Their writing states as fact that this passage allowed spousal abuse.[4]

A few scholars (writing in Hebrew) have posed an objection, albeit a simplistic one.[5] Far more, however, have accepted the aforementioned interpretation–even those who have noted that such a ruling is uncharacteristic of Maimonides, unprecedented in rabbinic literature, and ambiguous in practice.

How robust is the claim that Maimonides permitted husbands to hit wives? To answer that, we will now thoroughly examine the passage in question.

OVERALL CHARACTER OF THE MISHNEI TORAH

A defensible interpretation of any passage in the *Mishnei Torah* must take into account the nature, the style, and the goals of the book as a whole.

First of all, the *Mishnei Torah* is a restatement. Referring to it as the Compendium (*chibbur*) and a reformulation of "the entire Oral Torah," its editor claimed repeatedly that he did not add anything new to Jewish lore (beyond a few places where he explicitly said, "It seems to me . . ."). Later researchers have generally corroborated that claim. Hence, interpretation of the book ought to begin by presuming that its views are consistent with those of earlier teachers.

Paradoxically, for the sake of staying true to the content of the tradents, Maimonides often did not repeat them verbatim in his compilation. Rather, the editor synthesized into an artful mosaic nearly all of Jewish knowledge and belief as had been committed to writing in his day.[6] Thus, any one sentence may contain words whose source lies in several earlier works. Yet although he combined those words in novel ways, Maimonides claimed–and much research has since confirmed–that we can and should expect the result to be consistent with the prior material, and traceable to it. (While he knew that much of his audience wouldn't care about that traceability, he believed that it would be vital to scholars like himself.) Hence, an interpretation of the book should be able to correlate Maimonides' words with the earlier sources.

The second overall factor in interpretation is the style of writing. In this, the editor took as his model the Mishnah–the centerpiece text of rabbinic literature, completed nearly a thousand years before his time–which is a Hebrew characterized by pithiness and precision. Maimonides too strove for his work to be concise and amenable to memorization. This editor practiced what he preached: "In discussions of Torah and of wisdom, let a person's words be few, yet full of meaning" (*Deot* 2.4).[7] In the *Mishnei Torah*, as in the Mishnah, what is *not* stated is as meaningful as what is. A related attribute shared with the Mishnah is its intertextuality–allusions to other passages in either the same or in prior works; with these embedded "hyperlinks," verbiage was further compressed. As Twersky concluded, "careful attention to language is definitely woven into the fabric of Maimonides' codificatory achievement. Nothing about it is haphazard."[8]

Consequently, the *Mishnei Torah* is the kind of work whose text warrants a close and contextual reading, just as with the Mishnah (or the Bible, for that matter).[9] Because a given passage's meaning is not found in that passage alone, the act of reconstructing that meaning requires mining both the depth and breadth of the text. Those who look only to the words in front of them will not only be impoverished but also misled.

A further desideratum for interpretation is the editor's purpose for the book. In various writings, he related that one motive for composing his masterpiece was to further the moral and spiritual development of all Jews.[10] This creates a yardstick for the book's interpretation: How well does a given reading explain the passage in a manner that is consistent with this goal?

Maimonides' motive bears emphasis because the *Mishnei Torah* is so often referred to as a "law code." In fact, he believed that laws (and their study) were a tool for developing personal integrity–of perfecting body and soul; and so those concerns pervade the entire work. It's not accidental that he began this restatement of Jewish lore with a section on the recognition of spiritual reality and its implications, followed by a discourse on personal development–the self-regulation of one's emotional and ethical dispositions. Spiritual and ethical training are an integral part of what at first glance appears to be legal material.[11]

LEGAL BACKGROUND

As a restatement of more than a thousand years' worth of rabbinic teaching on all aspects of life, the *Mishnei Torah* expressed its ideas in terms of pre-existing categories of thought, terminology, and hypothetical cases. Therefore, to properly understand the *Mishnei Torah* and its formulations, it helps to look at prior works that Maimonides was responding to and summarizing: the halakhic (rabbinic legal) background of our passage.

In a tractate titled *Ketubot* (Marriage Contracts), the Mishnah had presented a model of how marriage is structured, in terms of the rights and duties of each party. (That model was elaborated upon soon thereafter in a related work, the Tosefta.) According to the model, the wife and husband form a partnership; the partnership is characterized by reciprocity and mutuality. To that end, the model imposes constraints on the will of each party. For a marriage to be viable, the wife cannot do whatever she wants–nor can the husband. In various cases of conflicting desires, the Mishnah explored *whose will should prevail*–in such a way as to maintain balance in the relationship.[12]

Because a main goal of the Mishnah was to generate thoughtful discussion, it was crafted literally to raise at least as many questions as it answered in the halakhic "rules" that it gave. The sages of the two Talmuds then took up the challenge to pose and elucidate many of those questions. Yet the Talmuds, too, were designed more to stimulate thinking than to define law and declare a subject closed; so they did not answer many questions definitively, either. However, they did refine the categories of discussion, and they explored various considerations that had only been implicit in Mishnah and Tosefta.

Primarily it was the world of the Mishnah, Tosefta, and Talmuds that Maimonides inhabited as he composed his *Mishnei Torah*. In the section titled *Ishut* (in which our passage appears), he methodically articulated the idealized model of marriage presented in those earlier works, while integrating the many facets of the arguments that they raised.

Like the classic literature, Maimonides presented marriage as being in part an economic partnership, including a predefined (and legally regulated) contribution of labor by the wife, in part to generate income for the household. (For a summary of the rabbinic economic model of marriage, see Excursus 1.) In addition, the model included a noneconomic category of wife's "work": acts that connote emotional and sexual intimacy–such things as making the bed, mixing his drinks, handing him small things that he asks for, and rinsing the dust off his feet. Some saw these acts as not compromising the husband's integrity, for temptations to infidelity might arise if someone else did these things for him. Others emphasized that they were vital opportunities to nurture marital intimacy.[13]

THE ISSUE AT STAKE

In *Ketubot* 5:7, after speaking of spousal duties, the Mishnah mentioned a category of spouse (female or male) called the Refuser.[14] The text didn't define the term, it simply prescribed a remedy. In this typically oblique manner, the Mishnah prompted the question of what it means when one party chooses not to carry out its duties. *When a wife reneges in participating fully in the partnership, what is the proper recourse?* This is the question that underlies our passage in § 21.10.[15]

Actually, that question has three parts, corresponding to the wife's three types of contracted work:

- What if the wife refuses to do income-producing work, while still expecting to receive salary and benefits from her husband? (Would it be fair for the husband to put her on unpaid leave? What if she then cannot afford to support herself? Should she be treated like a debtor?)
- What if she refuses to see to the management of the household– what if suddenly the flour is not being ground, the bread is not being baked, the clothes are not being washed, the infant is not being nursed, and the family's mount is not being fed? (Is she still entitled to receive her salary and benefits? What about engaging a re-

placement worker–for example, a domestic servant or a wetnurse? If so, which party should pay for this? How should the financing be arranged?)
- What if she refuses to perform the noneconomic tasks? (Again, what about hiring a replacement worker? Does that worker's gender matter?)[16]

THE EMOTIONAL DYNAMIC THAT FACES THE COURT

More fundamental–and only implicit in the early sources–is this question: what interpersonal emotional dynamic would lead to a wife's categorical refusal to work? Presumably it wouldn't be a matter of "going out on strike" for a higher salary or better benefits, because her legal rights (according to the model) imply that she could more effectively pursue such interests via a lawsuit as plaintiff rather than as defendant.

Nor would a wife's refusal to work mean that she wants out of the marriage. For the classic model–especially as conveyed by Maimonides–includes an arrangement wherein a wife can be granted an immediate divorce by declaring to the court that she's thoroughly disgusted with her husband.[17] If she wanted divorce, she would do better to take that route.

Rather, the category of Refuser seems to refer to a certain polarization within the marriage. As the Bible continually reiterates (starting with Adam and Eve!), human beings tend to avoid taking responsibility for their own emotional and spiritual well-being and destiny; and they almost relentlessly seek pretexts to justify that avoidance. Thus occurs a common pattern in a marriage: spouses convince themselves that they cannot get on with their own lives until their mate changes in some way; they each start trying to change their partner–who duly resists being made to change. And in one version of this dynamic, the husband takes on the role of authority figure while the wife takes on the role of rebel against authority. Both parties are trying to change the other but in reciprocally reactive ways.

Seen in this light, a wife's categorical refusal to work is designed to demonstrate–via an outrageous action that demands attention–that she has her own will and cannot be controlled by her spouse. In other words, she's caught up in resisting his goals for her. (Meanwhile, for his part, the husband is caught up in "correcting" his wife. However, it's her refusal that "grabs the headline," because hers is a more flamboyant act.)[18]

At this point, the case ends up in court. The identified problem is the wife's unwillingness to take responsibility. She has chosen to act within an arena that is at least partly economic; certain tasks *need to get done*– and that work has an economic value. Given the dynamics of the case, what sort of intervention should we expect?

Clearly, a coercive, authoritarian reaction by the court would only compound the polarization in the relationship. A heavy-handed resort to force would be counterproductive, furthering the wife's sense of victimization and resentment.

Intervention rather has three goals: resolve any urgent economic issues fairly; confront the wife directly with the logical consequences of her own dramatic irresponsibility; and prompt both parties to shift their focus–snapping the rigid dynamic.

THE PASSAGE IN QUESTION

Thus far we have established the following guidelines to interpretation:

- we can expect Maimonides' words to correlate with earlier rabbinic sources;
- a reading that disregards how the editor uses the same words elsewhere is likely to be inaccurate;
- the interpretation ought to be in accord with the express goals of the book; and
- the interpretation ought to bespeak a judicial intervention that productively addresses the underlying emotional dynamic.

Now we are ready to encounter our passage in the Mishnei Torah. The text appears to be stable across all extant manuscripts and printed editions; it reads as follows:

כל אשה שתמנע מלעשות מלאכה מן המלאכות שהיא חייבת לעשותן
כופין אותה ועושה אפילו בשוט.

Kol ishah she-timmana mi-laasot melakhah min ha-melakhot she-hi chayevet laasotan, kofin ot-ah ve-osah, afilu ve-shot.

Contemporary literature reflects a literal rendering, that of Rabbi Isaac Klein (cited in note 2) being typical: "A wife who refuses to perform any kind of work that she is obligated to do, may be compelled to perform it, even by scourging her with a rod." (The translator supplies the phrase "by scourging her," which is not in the Hebrew.) If this interpretation is accurate, it suggests that Maimonides understood that halakha (Jewish law) permitted a violent response, possibly by the husband.

Does this reading reflect the echoes of past rabbinic teachings, as expected? Does it accord with the words' meaning in the context of their usage elsewhere in the book? The answer is no on both counts, according to philological analyses of the sentence (Excursus 2) and its key term (Excursus 3). The results show that rabbinic source texts on domestic relations used these expressions figuratively, and also the *Mishnei Torah* used them figuratively. Both facts argue against reading § 21.10a literally.

Furthermore, the passage, according to its conventional interpretation, makes no contribution toward the book's goal of furthering the moral and spiritual development of both husband and wife. And its application would only intensify the case's underlying dynamic. For the husband in particular to be empowered to use force would violate one of the tenets of the rabbinic marriage model: "nobody can live in the same basket with a snake."[19]

What if we read our passage in a manner that understands its terms consistently with their meaning in rabbinic literature and in the *Mishnei Torah*? This yields the following plain-sense rendering:

> Any wife who refrains from doing work from among those tasks that she is obliged to do: we hold her to account, for her responsibility is to do the work. We get her attention via reproof and even via substantive (yet nonpunitive) interventions.

Such a reading leaves room for spiritual and moral development, and for productively resolving the conflict.

HOW THE PASSAGE FITS THE LEGAL HISTORY, INCLUDING MAIMONIDES' PREVIOUS WRITING

The conventional (literal) reading is inconsistent with halakha prior to Maimonides. To grasp that legal history, let us focus on R. Joseph Ibn Migash (Lucena, Spain, 1077-1141), a master teacher for Maimonides' father, who in turn was our editor's main teacher. Maimonides claimed to have made a special effort to collect the teachings of Ibn Migash (who published relatively little) and to put great store in his opinions. What did Ibn Migash teach on the case at hand?

In the Talmud of Babylonia, *Ketubot* 58b, one rabbi cites another rabbi to say: "[the husband] may hold his wife to [her commitment to do] income-producing work" (*yakhol le-khof-ah le-maaseh yadeha*). In a commentary on that complex passage, Ibn Migash concluded that this claim is indeed true–so long as the wife is maintained by her husband, although only up to the point that her income matches what other local women get for their work: *hu yakhol le-khof-ah she-taaseh lo shiur maaseh yadeha ho-iyl ve-nizonet mi-menu.*[20]

Further, Ibn Migash commented elsewhere on what to do in the event of her refusal. He held that a wife who refused work was so unlike a wife who refused sex as to require a different remedial approach. Writing in the customary Aramaic-Hebrew mix that comprised rabbinic legal jargon, he justified his conclusion on the grounds that with regard to work, the husband "has nearly all that creates the legal obligation in the matter" (*de-havei leih ke-khol mi she-mechayyev min ha-din ba-davar*).[21] That is, in the case of a work-refuser, the court holds the wife to the commitment she made upon marriage. (In contrast, when a wife categorically refuses sexual relations, the court only urges verbally that she relent, because a wife is not expected to engage in sexual relations against her will. In that case, the Mishnah's indirect remedy–progressively reducing her golden parachute [see Excursus 1]–is theoretically appropriate.) Therefore, explained Ibn Migash, the court may engage in a direct remedy: "we place her under the delinquent's ban (*shamta*)."[22]

In short, the legal issue was whether or not to employ the Mishnah's suggested remedy for a Refuser. Ibn Migash made a twofold reply. First, a wife could be held to her commitment to income-producing work, within reasonable limits. Second, in the eyes of the law, a work-refuser is different from a sex-refuser, such that some direct remedy (beyond reproof) is justified. Both points needed emphasis because the Talmud had left the matter unresolved.

As for Maimonides, given that he referred to this rabbi as "my teacher," we ought to expect that his writing would reflect these same ideas. And indeed it does. In a commentary on the Mishnah that Maimonides wrote as a prelude to the *Mishnei Torah*, he likewise held that remediation for a work-refuser should be handled differently: "However, if she does not want to do any [of the work] that a wife does for her husband, she is not a sex-refuser [whose will prevails]; rather, [we] hold her [to her (earlier) promise] (*kofin ot-ah*) in this matter, [and we resort to] any [direct] means of remediation [rather than only reproof or the Mishnah's specified procedure] (*kol minei khefiyyah*)."[23]

Regarding § 21.10a, if Maimonides' words there are read literally, then they both contradict his teacher and fail to restate his earlier point. However, if read figuratively, then–as one would expect–he makes the same necessary points as conveyed by his own earlier words and those of Ibn Migash.[24]

THE PASSAGE IN ITS IMMEDIATE LITERARY CONTEXT

Although we have just alluded to a judicial aspect to the situation, it has so far been only one of the levels on which our passage has operated–the same as throughout the *Mishnei Torah*, which assumes that persons may be held accountable for their actions before a court of law, and which was composed partly as a manual for judges. Now the text goes on to make the judicial aspect explicit. For it might happen that a husband asserts that the wife has not been doing the required work, yet she demurs from formally declaring refusal:

> He sues on the grounds that she is not doing [her work], whereupon she states that she is not refraining from doing [it]: we assign a woman or neighbors [to establish the facts] between them.[25] This case is [decided, after the facts are established] according to what the judge sees as possible [to accomplish].

> If it is established that the wife is refraining from work, then the court has flexibility in its choice of remedy. That is, the last sentence in § 21.10 applies to both parts of the passage: the setting is a lawsuit, a court case.[26]

Most published accounts of § 21.10a read it as permitting the husband to initiate violence.[27] Such a literal reading is incompatible with the judicial setting;[28] a figurative reading is not.

Widening the scope of the literary context slightly, let us look at the subsection immediately before § 21.10. It turns out that § 21.9, which is situated "while she was doing her work within her home," is the reciprocal mate of § 21.10, which takes place while she is *not* doing her work within her home. Now, § 21.9 clearly reflects a balance of the two party's competing interests: a wife is exempt from liability for damage to her husband's property; he must accept any losses. Why? For the sake of the smooth functioning of the household and to avoid strife, says the text explicitly. And from the literary link between the two subsections, we can expect the same spirit of mutuality in § 21.10.[29] Again, a literal reading of § 21.10a is incompatible with that theme; a figurative reading is not.

THE CASE FOR A READING OF ABUSE IN § 21.10A

What published evidence supports the conventional (literal) reading that Maimonides is permitting wife-battering?

Of the seventeen writers cited (note 2), only two present actual arguments. Both of those researchers dwell on the question of who "compels" the wife–is it the husband or the court? Both find the passage ambiguous on this score.[30] To resolve the apparent ambiguity, they investigate how other medieval rabbinic authorities handled the passage. The logic is this: we defer to the expertise of rabbis who in general understood the *Mishnei Torah* well, and thus can be relied upon to tell us what Maimonides' words meant. After finding that other Rishonim (leading rabbis of the 12th-14th centuries) believed that Maimonides was allowing a husband to beat his wife, both researchers conclude that it's what our passage means.

This approach faces certain pitfalls, so the next section will assess how well the adduced texts support the case. But before proceeding to that issue, it should be noted that proponents of the "wife-beating" interpretation can still do much in the way of analysis of our passage on its own terms, so as to bolster their case directly.[31] See Excursus 4.

INTERPRETATIONS BY MEDIEVAL AUTHORITIES

In order for an imputed meaning (that is, the meaning according to a later rabbinic author) to be valid, it must be shown that the rabbi's writing was free of other agendas that would distort his assessment of § 21.10a. Furthermore, his later explanation must itself be unambiguous. (Otherwise, any interpretation offered is contaminated by either the eisegetic abilities–or if you prefer, the psychic projections–of the medieval rabbi, or the contemporary researcher, or both.) If these methodological criteria are not met, then a given interpretation can be considered little more than speculation.[32]

What scholars have cited to establish that "Maimonides permitted wife-beating" are texts by six prominent rabbis: a gloss (*hassagah*) on the *Mishnei Torah*, by Abraham ben David (RaBaD) of Posquieres (12th century);[33] a hortatory tract (*Iggeret ha-Teshuvah*) by Jonah ben Abraham of Gerona (13th century);[34] a comment (*chiddush*) on the Talmud, by Moses Nahmanides (RaMBaN) of Barcelona (13th century);[35] a comment (*chiddush*) on the Talmud, by Menahem ben Solomon Meiri don Vidal of Perpignan (13th century);[36] a comment (*chiddush*) on the Talmud, by Solomon Ibn Adret (RaShBA) of Barcelona (c. 1300);[37] a responsum by RaShBA (c. 1300);[38] a comment on the *Mishnei Torah*, in *Maggid Mishnah*, by Vidal Yom Tov of Tolosa (14th century).[39] Let's examine these sources in light of the above criteria.[40]

First, RaBaD's terse remark is ambiguous on several levels.[41] Thus, it is of little help in confidently establishing what Maimonides meant.

Second, it has yet to be shown that the work by Jonah Gerondi, or RaShBA's responsum, anywhere mentions or even alludes to *Ishut* § 21.10a. Although they do say that a husband may theoretically be exempt from prosecution after hitting his wife, the special circumstances that they cite do *not* involve a wife's refusal to work. Thus, it appears that both of these works had another agenda–and that they shed no light on Maimonides.

Third, RaMBaN and RaShBA did both paraphrase the characteristic language of § 21.10a, but they placed it in a court context; arguably, too, their usage reflected a figurative–rather than literal–understanding of Maimonides. RaMBaN was explaining a passage in Talmud,[42] while RaShBA was collating the statements of various Rishonim with a talmudic opinion.[43] Not only do these passages have another agenda, but also they are ambiguous–if not actually contrary to the claim being made.

Fourth, Meiri at first glance does portray § 21.10a as referring to direct and violent action by the husband. At the same time, he exaggerates (one might even say: caricatures) the position of *all* of the sources that he cites in this passage–which suggests that he's intentionally doing the same to Maimonides–apparently for rhetorical effect.[44] Later on, at any rate, he treats those opinions (which include nonviolent, court-imposed measures) as different ways of saying the same thing.[45] This implies that he was not taking those earlier formulations literally–which perhaps explains why he felt free to exaggerate their language.

Lastly, Yom Tov's comment on § 21.10a can be understood as showing how other authorities (the Talmud commentaries of RaMBaN and

RaShBA mentioned above) later employed its characteristic phrase figuratively. Moreover, it can be interpreted as asserting that the main issue in § 21.10a is the distinction between responses for the case of a work-refusing versus a sex-refusing wife–i.e., that it doesn't address when violence might be warranted, nor who might be the one to administer it. The comment is ambiguous at best.

In short, *all of these sources fail the validity test.* Consequently, we are left with nothing substantial or compelling to back up the claim that later rabbis believed that *Ishut* § 21.10a referred to a husband's literal use of a switch. And thus the modern and widespread claim that Maimonides accepted wife-beating is left without support–other than what a cursory and hyperliteral reading of the passage might suggest.

SUMMARY OF FINDINGS

Although conventional wisdom holds that Maimonides permitted a husband to beat his wife if she failed to do her housework, supporting evidence for that view is surprisingly sparse.

The common interpretation of § 21.10a fails all tests: It does not accord with the nature, style, or goal of the *Mishnei Torah*. It is inconsistent with the dynamics of the case, with the prior usage of the key terms in halakhic literature and in the book itself, and with the thread of ongoing legal discussions. Nor does it suit the immediate literary context. And it has yet to be confirmed by the readings of other early medieval authorities. On all counts, it is a stretch.

In contrast, a figurative reading of Maimonides' words seems to meet all the criteria considered (although it could still be wrong, of course). Furthermore, it implicitly takes a stand *against* spousal abuse. For by expecting a discontented husband to resort to a lawsuit–and by containing nothing to justify wife-battering–§ 21.10 means that the case of a work-refusing wife must be addressed in light of Maimonides' default position that spousal assault, battery, and injury are each prosecutable offenses.[46]

In conclusion, *the "fact" that Maimonides condoned spousal abuse is uncertain at best.* While the conventional wisdom may be correct, the case is far from proven, and much evidence actually points in the other direction.

WHAT CAN WE LEARN FROM CONVENTIONAL WISDOM?

That so many modern scholars have put their faith in a "fact" with so little to support it–this is in itself a phenomenon worthy of reflection: What is it that prompts people to firmly believe facts with little justification? What fuels the popularity of the view that Maimonides condoned wife-battering? Here let me offer three possible responses, with brief remarks, for your consideration.

In some cases, perhaps, authors have innocently repeated the claim as made by others who have credentials. The present case may then serve as a reminder of the pitfalls of doing so.

Another factor that may condition one's attachment to a particular reading of *Ishut* § 21.10a is one's emotional stance regarding the premodern world (including its patriarchal impulses). It would be natural enough for those who find safety in the modern world to then view the words of Maimonides–a towering symbol of the premodern world–as a lightning rod.

What may be the most pervasive factor emerges from noting that § 21.10a contains violent language (whether it be understood literally or figuratively): violence tends to be unsettling and thus can distort both perception and logic. Happily, determining an accurate reading of texts like this is a worthwhile exercise. For the more we cultivate our ability to encounter such texts with presence of mind and emotional neutrality, the better we are able to confront real violence in our own lives. (And vice versa.) *Let that holy work continue!*

Excursus 1. Rabbinic Economic Model of Marriage: More Familiar Than You Think

As I read the source texts and Maimonides' economic model of marriage, the closest analogy in our contemporary society is today's *employer-employee* relationship.[47] The model in effect gives the husband the role of entrepreneur. As "employer," he offers his spouse a weekly salary, plus substantial fringe benefits: comprehensive health insurance; weekly survivor benefits (for her daughters); life insurance (for her sons); kidnapping insurance (that is, guaranteed ransom payment in case of brigands, pirates, and the like); burial insurance; and a golden parachute (*ikar ketubah*). In addition, the model specifies not only a minimum wage but also regulates the benefits; beyond those thresholds, the salary and bonuses are expected to be commensurate with the husband's wealth.

In consideration for receiving the above, the wife as "employee" offers her spouse the proceeds from her skilled labor (typified by spinning wool into yarn), and she takes responsibility for certain kinds of ongoing work. Some of this work is what we think of today as "household chores," but other parts involve what many people today look to a supermarket, gas station, and a fast-food restaurant to provide–namely, milled flour, baked bread, a ready vehicle, and cooked meals. (Back then, most people worked at home: the household was where most of society's goods and services were produced.)

The wife may choose to become self-employed if she wishes–that is, if she believes that she has the means to support herself and is willing to take the risk. If so, she keeps her own earnings and receives no salary or benefits from her husband.[48]

In various ways, the model proceeds to constrain what the "boss" can legitimately ask of his "employee," in order that she maintain her dignity and not be exploited. For example, her quota for producing marketable goods is regulated by local custom regarding what wives do.

Excursus 2. Translation: The Idiom and the Odyssey

The heart of the matter–the operative clause–is *kofin ot-ah ve-osah, afilu ve-shot*. Let's look at each element in turn.

The Absent Subject. The subject of the plural verb *kofin* is only implied. In Hebrew, first-person and third-person participle inflections have the same form, so the intended subject is either a "we" or a "they"–but who? Given that this style was typical of the Mishnah's rhetoric too, the *lack* of specificity should be construed as meaningful: the subject is intentionally amorphous.

Indeed, it is a rhetorical play. The implied subject of both the Mishnah and Maimonides is actually the reader–who is being called to join the ongoing conversation; it is the immediate "we" of the study hall, the "we" that creates a community.[49]

Kofin ot-ah. The verb *kofin* is common throughout the Mishnah's discussion of the institution of marriage, picked up and used often in the Tosefta and Talmuds as well. Although usually translated "compel" or "force," such renderings can be misleading in halakhic discussion of marriage, where *kofin* is a legal technical term.[50] For what's exerting the "pressure" is *the situation*, that is, the institution of marriage as defined by the legal model: when parties marry, they tacitly agree to certain expectations that are spelled out in advance in these texts. Thus, neither the reader, husband, wife, or court need to literally apply pressure or coercion; the verb's usage is figurative.

Maimonides uses *kofin* in the exact same way, as a figure of speech. In *Ishut*, the term *kofin* appears thirty times, and in two-thirds of those instances it serves to constrain the husband's will rather than the wife's will.

In this particular case, *ot-ah* ("her") is clearly the verb's direct object, so that what *kofin ot-ah* means here is that her will is not followed (unlike the similar case in § 14.8-14). Or, using an analogous English trope: "[we] hold her [to account]"–which, if taken literally, would also sound violent (as if "hold" meant grabbing her body without her consent).

Ve-osah. Literally, "and [she] does," that is, "for she should do [the work]"–it is her responsibility. (It could also mean "so that she does [the work]," but the rest of the analysis suggests an emphasis more on process than on outcome.)

Afilu. This adverb *afilu* ("even") is an intensive to convey that the term that follows (*ve-shot*) is not the first resort: start with remonstrations and then move to *ve-shot* remedies.[51]

Ve-shot. The modifier *ve-shot* literally means "with a switch" (that is, a flexible twig, rod, or whip). *Shot* is an unusual and therefore specialized term. In biblical Hebrew, it referred to a device used to *command attention and interrupt unresponsiveness by stinging*–and not to cause lasting pain or injury, nor to punish.[52]

The term is not used at all in either Mishnah or Tosefta.

In the two Talmuds, it appears only once in a halakhic context (*Ketubot* 77a-b).[53] At issue is how far the court should go in prompting a husband to divorce his wife (when that outcome is deemed necessary). There, chastising him with *shotei* (plural of *shot*) is counterposed with verbal chastisement: the choice is either "with words" or "with switches." The Sages of course knew that other means of persuasion were available besides those two! Thus, "with switches" was a figure of speech (specifically, a synecdoche) wherein "switches" represented the court's entire repertoire of nonverbal interventions. Because a switch is a concrete term that gets people's attention, it was employed figuratively in the discussion, to heighten the rhetorical effect.

This case is about inducement, not punishment. To paraphrase Rabbi Abba in that passage, the intent was this: a resistant husband is temporarily a slave to his passions; what's needed is an intervention that jars the man's perception so that he sees the bigger picture and remembers his real priorities.[54]

That lone, yet dramatic, legal usage of the word *shot* becomes a trope in rabbinic discussions of court remedies.[55]

In short, in rabbinic literature, *shot* is used figuratively. It fits a context where inducement is the goal; and it means "substantive measures"–as opposed to reproof.

Maimonides uses *shot* in just one other place in *Ishut*, to restate the talmudic case: *kofin oto u-makkin oto be-shot* (literally, "we force him and beat him with a switch"; § 15.7). There he adds a crucial verb, *makkin* (beat), to what would otherwise have read *kofin oto . . . ve-shot*, an exact parallel to the wording in § 21.10a. The difference is telling. One might assume that in § 15.7 the word *makkin* is superfluous, but that is contrary to how *Mishnei Torah* is supposed to be read (see section 2). Playing by the rules of the game, we must conclude that the two key terms in § 21.10a (*kofin . . . ve-shot*) do not by themselves convey actual hitting; the expression is figurative.[56]

Excursus 3. Why Did Maimonides Prefer to "Switch" Than Fight?

The conventional reading of our passage understands the term *shot* literally as a weapon. Yet the word's very rarity in Maimonides' work and in rabbinic literature (see Excursus 2) is a sure sign to the reader that it bears a special (figurative) meaning. That is, its figurative sense is protected by its not being the usual word used to name an implement for striking.

But that's not all. With regard to implements for striking, rabbinic literature also offered Maimonides four other terms: *retzua, chevel, shevet,* and *pizra* (Rashi: *makkel*). These would have been far better terms to convey either a husband's or a court's use of force–had that been the editor's intent–for they already bear strong connotations of that type.[57] Compared to *shot* this is a "striking" difference that further argues against a literal reading.

Moreover, a term conspicuous here by its absence is *makkat mardut* (disciplinary flogging), which a court employs when offenders resist doing their duty.[58] The expression *makkin oto makkat mardut* (beat him with disciplinary flogging) appears more than a hundred times in the *Mishnei Torah*–three of them in *Ishut*–but not here.[59] If Maimonides had thought that the wife should literally be flogged, he could easily have said so. This further suggests that his goal here was not to physically force the wife to relent.[60]

Maimonides may have been the first to employ the term *ve-shot* in connection with a wife's refusing to work. Yet its use is consistent with his editorial approach. Succinct and easy to remember, the term conveys a unique, precise, and relevant talmudic connotation.

Excursus 4. Recipe for Establishing that Maimonides Condoned Wife-Beating

To prove the existence in our passage of a husband's license to abuse, mix together the following ingredients: show how that reading fits the book's overall nature, style, and goals; show how it matches the usage of terms in halakhic literature and in the book; show how it matches the dynamics of the case; and show it suits the immediate literary context. Combine the mixture with an explanation of how it does these things more elegantly and plausibly than the alternative explanation presented in this article. Garnish with answers to the following questions. *Serve chilled.*

1. How is a literal reading of § 21.10a compatible with the model of marriage that Maimonides constructed incrementally throughout *Ishut?*[61]
2. On what grounds can and should *kofin* be interpreted in § 21.10a to refer to the husband, as opposed to similar cases where *kofin* clearly does *not* refer to the husband?[62]
3. On what grounds can the word "scourging" or "whipping" or "beating" or "flogging" be supplied in translating § 21.10a, given that any such verb is conspicuous by its absence there?[63]
4. What is the source in rabbinic tradition for this supposed teaching of Maimonides? (So far as I know, none of several qualified researchers has been able to clearly identify such a source–nor even a good hint.[64])

NOTES

1. Although repeatedly denied, spousal violence has long been part of the fabric of Jewish life. (For evidence based on early medieval victims' testimony and corroborated by rabbinic courts, see my "Initiatives to Address Physical Violence by Jewish Husbands, 218 b.c.e.-1400 c.e.," *JORA* 2/3 [2001], pp. 25-49.) The present article proceeds to consider the opposite phenomenon, the "flip side" of denial: a tendency to perceive spousal abuse in texts where it may not actually be present.

2. At the same time, this masterpiece has always been controversial, for many reasons. The literature on it is enormous; see, for example, Joseph Kafach's preface (Hebrew) to *Mishnei Torah* (1983), and Isadore Twersky, *Introduction to the Code of Maimonides*, New Haven: Yale, 1980.

3. The list includes, in reverse chronological order:

Elliot N. Dorff,* *Love Your Neighbor and Yourself: A Jewish Approach to Modern Personal Ethics* (Philadelphia: JPS, 2003), 159, 289 n. 14

Carol Goodman Kaufman,* *Sins of Omission: The Jewish Community's Reaction to Domestic Violence* (Boulder, CO: Westview, 2003), p. 64

Emily Taitz,* Sondra Henry, and Cheryl Tallan, "Jewish Women Under Islam," *The JPS Guide to Jewish Women* (Philadelphia: JPS, 2003), 67-68, 289

Elliot N. Dorff, "Aspects of Judaism and Family Violence," *Embracing Justice: A Resource Guide for Rabbis on Domestic Abuse*, ed. Diane Gardsbane (Washington, DC: Jewish Women International, 2002), 45

Elliot N. Dorff, "Family Violence (HM 424.1995)," *Responsa, 1991-2000: The Committee on Jewish Law and Standards of the Conservative Movement* (NY: Rabbinical Assembly, 2002), 776-77

Gus Kaufman, Jr.,* Wendy Lipschutz, and Drorah O'Donnell Setel, "Responding to Domestic Violence," *Jewish Pastoral Care: A Practical Handbook from Traditional and Contemporary Sources* (Woodstock, VT: Jewish Lights, 2001), 239-40

Naomi Graetz,* *Silence Is Deadly: Judaism Confronts Wifebeating* (Northvale, NJ: Jason Aronson, 1998), pp. 104-106

Dov Rappel, *Ha-Rambam Ke-Mechanekh* (Jerusalem: Yediot Acharonot, 1997), 122

Elliot N. Dorff, "In God's Image: Aspects of Judaism Relevant to Family Violence," *Resource Guide for Rabbis on Domestic Violence* (Jewish Women International, 1996), 94

Avraham Grossman,* "Medieval Rabbinic Views on Wife-Beating, 800-1300," *Jewish History* 5/1 (Spring 1991), 56 [but see below, note 30]

Aviva Cantor, *Jewish Women/Jewish Men: The Legacy of Patriarchy in Jewish Life* (Harper-SanFrancisco, 1995), 130

Joseph Telushkin, *Jewish Literacy* (NY: William Morrow and Co., 1991), 487

Mordechai Frishtik, "Violence Against Women in Judaism," *Journal of Psychology & Judaism* 14 (Fall 1990), 137

Debra Orenstein, "How Jewish Law Views Wife Beating," *Lilith* 20 (Summer 1988), 9

Julie Ringold Spitzer, *When Love is Not Enough: Spousal Abuse in Rabbinic and Contemporary Judaism* (NY: Women of Reform Judaism, 1985; rev. 1991), 11-12, 17

Rachel Biale, *Women and Jewish Law* (NY: Schocken, 1984; rev. 1995), 94-95

Samuel Morrell, "An Equal or a Ward: How Independent is a Married Woman According to Rabbinic Law?" *Jewish Social Studies* XLIV (Summer-Fall 1982), 198

S. D. Goitein, *A Mediterranean Society*, 6 vols. (Berkeley: Univ. of Calif., 1976), viii, C, 1 = vol. 3, 185

Isaac Klein, "Introduction," *The Code of Maimonides. Book 4: The Book of Women* (New Haven: Yale, 1972), xxxv

Louis Jacobs, "Woman," *Encyclopaedia Judaica* (1971), 16:627

Meir Havazelet, "The Husband's Participation in Corporal Punishment of His Wife" [Hebrew], appendix to Chaim Tykocinski's *Takkanot Ha-Geonim* (NY: Yeshiva University, 1959), 132

*I thank these authors for privately challenging my thinking on the topic of this article while encouraging me to develop and publish my own view. Also deserving of thanks for those reasons are Carole Stein, Marcia Cohn Spiegel, and Rabbis Gail Diamond, Robert Gluck, Vivian Mayer, Yaakov Menken, and Avi Shafran.

4. Some authors have made their point only by implication (e.g., Goitein). See also note 30.

5. Kafach, *loc. cit.*; Nachum Rabinovitch, ed., *Mishnei Torah* (Jerusalem: Maaliyot, 1990), *loc. cit.* (449). They maintain that Maimonides' use of a plural verb inflection (see Excursus 2) refers to the court and not the husband. However, this argument is not conclusive, partly because the legal literature both before and after Maimonides often couches the matter (and even restates his position) using the singular, as we shall see. Grossman cites both of these authors in explaining why he has reconsidered his position; see note 30.

6. Twersky, *op. cit.*, 346, 51. He adds: "Maimonides could and did fuse words, phrases, and fragments of multiple documents into one unified seamless formulation" (52-53). See also Menahem Elon, "Codification of Law," *Encyclopaedia Judaica* 5:639-641.

7. All translations in this article are by its author.

8. Twersky, *op. cit.*, 354.

9. Considerations of this particular book aside, let's recall that the rabbinic enterprise presumes that word choice *matters*. The Midrash is the record of rabbis pointing to the nuances of biblical word choice; the Talmud is filled with rabbis scrutinizing the wording of other rabbis' statements.

10. See discussion in Twersky, 61 ff.

11. Twersky concludes: "His aim was to . . . provide knowledge, understanding, and even inspiration, and not merely to summarize practical conclusions and obligatory instructions . . . The best way to approach Maimonides is to view him as a scholar vigorously pursuing and creatively uniting two inseparable disciplines [namely, law and philosophy]" (78, 509).

12. Today, partisans (typically: Orthodox vs. feminist) debate whether the rabbinic model of marriage is good or bad for women. In my view, this is a displacement issue that unduly divides contemporary Jews. If spouses are behaving responsibly, the model works fine; if spouses aren't behaving responsibly, changing the system will not help. (That's why spousal abuse exists in egalitarian households as well as in Orthodox ones.)

13. *Ishut* §§ 21.3-4, 7-8; see also Maimonides' *Commentary on the Mishnah, Ketubot* 5:5. His sources appear to be Talmud of the Land of Israel, *Ketubot* 5:5; and Talmud of Babylonia, *Kiddushin* 70a. (Note that in the rabbinic marriage model, the sexual relationship per se is treated as an entirely separate category of mutual responsibility.) That Maimonides was knowingly describing an idealized, heuristic model of marriage is supported by its being somewhat at odds with the historical reconstruction based on the myriad Geniza documents from his own time and place. See Goitein, *op. cit.*, I:127-29; III:132-33, 341-33, 359.

14. Hebrew, *moredet* (f.) and *mored* (m.). The conventional, literal rendering as "rebel" is mechanical and doesn't fit this context; that English word connotes forceful opposition and lack of success, neither of which is inherently applicable here. Further, in the rabbinic model of domestic relations, rebellion alone does not count; the label of *moredet* or *mored* applies only after an explicit public declaration of refusal. Additionally, the most common denotation of "rebel"–to disobey an authority figure–is clearly out of place when speaking of a *mored*. In contrast, rendering as "refuser" works for both genders, which is a proper reflection of the Mishnaic construction of the issue.

15. Elsewhere in chapter 21, Maimonides treats corresponding questions of what's at stake when the husband refuses to do his part.

16. Some feminists may feel that the work-refusing wife deserves cheers for resisting what they see as rabbinic law's near-slavery of women. Arguably, however, challenging the wife to fulfill her commitments might do her more to promote her moral development. Some might retort, "He's a grown man–let him rinse his own feet!" But such actions, practical in their time and place, are also symbolic. Contemporary egalitarian equivalents might include giving a shoulder-rub (after a long day's work) or checking our partner's body for ticks (after a forest hike). What does it mean when we're *not* willing to do these things for our partner?

17. *Ishut* § 14.8. There Maimonides famously remarks, "For [a wife] is not like a captive that she must engage in sexual relations with someone whom she loathes."

18. Physical violence may well be an avenue of expression in these arguments–possibly going both ways. (The conflictual dynamic described here is akin to the stereotypical teenage rebellion against parents. It is different than when a tyrannical husband consistently or cyclically beats a compliant wife, which is what most contemporary observers mean by "spousal abuse.") If so, then (according to the rabbinic model) such assault, battery, or injury is handled as a separate claim–if either party chooses to make the violence an issue; see *Mishnei Torah, Chovel u-Mazzik*, chaps. 2-5.

19. A proverb featured in the Talmud of Babylonia, *Ketubot* 86b, and frequently in domestic-relations literature thereafter. It precludes actions (including violence) that betray the basic trust underlying a viable marriage; see Tosafot *Ketubot* 62b s.v. "Rav Huna."

20. As adduced in R. Menahem Meiri, *Beit ha-Bechirah* on *Ketubot*, p. 235 (Sofer edition, Jerusalem 5702), as quoted in Rabinovitch, *op. cit.*, 448-49.

21. As adduced in *Shitah Mekubbetzet, Ketubot* 63a; I was not able to find R. Ibn Migash's talmudic comments firsthand. Ibn Migash is explaining the *Sefer ha-Halakhot* of his teacher, R. Isaac Alfasi (Fez and Lucena, 1013-1103), *Ketubot* 26b, on the Talmud of Babylonia's 63a. Ibn Migash cited R. Hai Gaon (Pumbedita, served 998-1038) as having made the same point as Alfasi, about a century earlier. This claim correlates with the like-minded responsum by Hai Gaon's father that will be considered shortly.

22. As presented in the classic sources and in the *Mishnei Torah*, a delinquent's ban (*shamta* or *niddui*) was available to confront a delinquent with the consequences of her (or his) irresponsibility, such as nonpayment of a debt. Like anyone declared a delinquent, a wife under the ban would have been expected to live in a state of mourning: neither bathing (except for rinsing her face, hands, and feet), cutting her hair, laundering her clothes, nor wearing shoes; and she would have lived in confinement with her family, without receiving visitors or engaging in outside conversation except for business purposes. A ban lasted for 30 days (or until redress occurred) and was renewable. See *Mishnei Torah, Talmud Torah* § 6.14 and chap. 7.
Rabbi Ibn Migash's approach is consistent with a responsum that the authoritative Rav Sherira Gaon issued a century earlier in Babylonia. Sherira Gaon (Pumbedita, served 968-1006) had been asked to address only a wife's domestic-production tasks, such as milling flour and baking bread. He opined that "the husband has [the right] to insist that she do tasks that she is obliged to [do]" (*mihu iyt la-baal le-mikhpiyyah le-maavad melakhot de-michayyeva bahi*); and therefore "if he petitions the court to place her under the delinquent's ban until she does [the work], we do so." *Otzar ha-Geonim, Ketubot* 59b, #429, pp. 170-171. (I thank Avraham Grossman for calling this responsum to my attention.) On this responsum, see further at the end of note 50.

23. *Ketubot* 5:7, which I have rendered idiomatically from R. Joseph Kafach's Hebrew translation from Maimonides' original Arabic.

24. We saw above that in his treatment of the issue, Maimonides' "teacher," Ibn Migash, had recommended a delinquent's ban. Maimonides himself (according to a figurative reading) chose language that, while consistent with Ibn Migash's teaching, is more general. Why? Several considerations could have prompted Maimonides to adopt language that bespoke a range of responses. They include:

1. *The wife's "intimate" (noneconomic) tasks*: it's not clear that Ibn Migash had those in mind in his discussion of a work-refusing wife. Maimonides, however, strongly worded within the same chapter a prohibition that the wife not delegate those tasks to servants (both at Mishnah *Ketubot* 5:5 and *Ishut* § 21.4; cf. Talmud of the Land of Israel, *Ketubot* 5:6 [33b]). I speculate that with regard to those tasks, Maimonides believed that a delinquent's ban was inappropriate. (Meanwhile, he might have agreed with other authorities who reasoned that for economic tasks, direct remediation–such as hiring a servant–might be better than a ban.)

2. *The court's role in resolving the case*: A show of outside "pressure" can sometimes enable opposing parties to climb out of their entrenched positions while still saving face. But what is appropriate "pressure" depends on the particulars.

25. In § 21.10b, the court first establishes whether or not the wife is actually fulfilling her duty. (Maimonides suggests a female witness not as a gesture of sympathy to the wife; rather, in the classic rabbinic model it would be unthinkable to put a male alone in the house with her.) This resort to witnesses does not apply to the case in § 21.10a, where all parties agree that the wife refuses to work.

26. Nahum Rabinovitch made a similar point, *op. cit.*

27. According to another literal interpretation (see note 5), the text refers to a beating imposed by the court.

28. For another literal reading that at first glance is compatible with the judicial setting, see note 30.

29. Similarly, the following passage, §§ 21.11-13, also reflects a nuanced balance of the spouses' competing interests. By interpolation, § 21.10 should match the theme.

30. Naomi Graetz tacitly admits that she found Maimonides' words ambiguous, for she asks rhetorically regarding the wife, "Who compels her?" but never answers that question in terms of the text itself (*op. cit.*, 105). Avraham Grossman, who in 1991 had perceived in our passage "the husband's right to beat his wife" and translated *ve-shot* as "by means of whipping" (*op. cit.*), now thinks it unlikely that the husband was the intended subject ("Violence Against Women [chap. 10]," *Pious and Rebellious: Jewish Women in Europe in the Middle Ages* [Hebrew] (Jerusalem: Zalman Shazar Center for Jewish History, 2001; rev. 2003), 382-388, 554. Both authors posit without evidence–but with alarm, because of the supposed "opening" that it would give abusive husbands–that what Maimonides may intend is that the court gives the husband permission to go home and compel his wife via blows (Graetz, *ibid.*; Grossman, 380 and personal communication). Apparently this same reading was tacitly assumed by at least two authors before them. Spitzer (*op. cit.*) rendered *kofin otah* as "the Beit Din [court] should compel her," yet she concluded that this ruling permitted a woman to be beaten "by her husband." Likewise, Frishtik (*op. cit.*) wrote: "According to Maimonides, it is permissible to beat one's wife"; but after adducing § 21.10, he hastened to explain: "Compelling her . . . is not the responsibility of her husband, but of a rabbinic court." In other words, the court empowers the husband to "whip" her.

However, in the classic rabbinic model, when it comes to settling disputes, a local court's main role is to serve as an honest broker, inducing the parties to negotiate a reconciliation (*pesharah*). (See, e.g., *Mishnei Torah, Sanhedrin* § 22.4. For more on early medieval court procedure–including a flow chart–see my previous *JORA* article, *op. cit.*, 36-8, 40.) The above interpretation of § 21.10 is thus at odds with the court's function as portrayed by the model. Meanwhile, if (as I contend) no literal "whipping" is involved in § 21.10, then the whole question of who administers it is moot.

31. Some scholars have objected to reading figuratively, arguing that because Maimonides was writing for a general audience, and because a typical reader would take the expressions in question literally, then he must have meant his words literally (Grossman and Taitz, personal communications). I disagree. Practically speaking, he could not define (nor erase) every figure of speech in an age-old legal literature. Granted that they do bear some risk of being misunderstood. But that does not relieve the reader of responsibility for reckoning with them. In the end, in order to derive the plain sense, one must always read contextually.

32. Paradigmatic unbiased evidence would be a responsum (*teshuvah*), authored by a jurisconsult for a real (not hypothetical) case that involved wife-beating, who did not have a personal stake in the outcome of the case, and who discussed § 21.10a explicitly. Standing in contrast as an example of writing with another agenda is the genre of Talmud commentary. At best, such a work is like a law review article discussing hypothetical situations; as any attorney or halakhist knows, such musings shouldn't be confused with legal advice for actual cases, let alone with a verdict handed down by a judge in a court of law. More often, however, a Talmud commentary is simply trying to reconcile apparent contradictions in the text of the Talmud itself–while collating the opinions of other commentators on those same issues. Regarding domestic violence, the "problem" is that a husband's alleged right to beat his wife is nowhere discussed in the Talmud (rather, it is implicitly denied); not surprisingly, contemporary researchers have so far failed to find talmudic commentators among the Rishonim who addressed that subject directly.

33. Literally: "I've never heard of chastisement via switches for wives [or: women]" (*loc. cit.*).

34. Graetz cites p. 11 of *Iggeret ha-Teshuvah* in both its first and second printed editions.

35. *Chiddushim, Ketubot* 63a. Graetz and Grossman refer to this passage by citing only its excerpt in *Maggid Mishnah, loc. cit.* (see below), not realizing its original source. The brief quotation within the later work admits of their interpretation but does not prove it, while the fuller (and less ambiguous) text argues against it.

36. *Op. cit*, pp. 249-50, 259-60.

37. *Chiddushim, Ketubot* 64a, s.v. *u-le-inyan pesak halakhah ba-moredet* (p. 194). Graetz and Grossman refer to this passage by citing only its excerpt in *Maggid Mishnah, loc. cit.* The critique in note 35 also applies here.

38. Graetz adduces 7:477 and #102 of *Responsa Attributed to RaMBaN*, which she sees as two versions of the same responsum (108-9).

39. *Loc. cit*

40. Significantly, neither Graetz nor Grossman have pointed to any rabbinic authority who explicitly cited Maimonides' opinion in favor of his own view that wife-beating was *acceptable* (and indeed most of them *explicitly opposed* wife-beating).

41. Modern scholars confidently state what RaBaD meant, yet they disagree! Contrast, e.g., Rappel's view (*op. cit.*, 122) with that of Graetz (*op. cit.*, 176, 203), and both of those with that of Grossman (*Pious and Rebellious*, 384, 388). Unrecognized is just how ambiguous RaBaD's laconic gloss is. Did he understand *ve-shot* literally or figuratively? Is he even judging the appropriateness of *ve-shot* to this particular situation? (After all, the main goal of Ravad's *hassagot* was to illuminate Maimonides' sources and point to alter-

native opinions in the halakhic literature. See Kafach, *op. cit.*, and Isadore Twersky, *Rabad of Posquieres* [Cambridge: Harvard, 1962].) And regarding who supposedly applies "persuasion" to the wife (the "husband or court?" question), his words can be read either way (or even that he saw no need to differentiate). To grasp what RaBaD is saying, one would need to check against his other writings–particularly his *hassagot* to Alfasi, which dwell on the question of a work-refusing versus a sex-refusing wife–and against his opinion as recorded by his students. This basic effort has yet to be reported in the literature that I'm aware of.

42. RaMBaN's explicit agenda was this question: "I wonder how it is that we hold that [the wife] is not [treated in the same way as] a sex-refuser." He did not address a contemporary question like Grossman's: "To whom is given the authority . . . to strike the wife . . .–to the husband or to the court?"

43. Ibn Adret portrayed this hypothetical case as being initiated "when she says, 'I will not do [the work]'." This has the ring of a formal declaration in court (or in front of witnesses). As with RaMBaN, his main issue was whether or not a work-refuser is to be treated like a sex-refuser. That he understood *ve-shot* figuratively is evidenced by the way he (arguably) used it to describe both of the two practical (typical and converse) options that he discussed: either the husband does not maintain the work-refuser, or else the court ensures that he gets hired help at her expense. (He also seems to have used *ve-shot* figuratively in his comment on *Ketubot* 61b, s.v. *Rabbi Yosé*; p. 190, top.) Neither remedial option is a punishment; rather, they are logical consequences of the wife's refusal; by either means, her wish not to work is respected while the husband's interests are addressed.

44. Similarly, Meiri uses exaggerated, superlative epithets for his sources, rather than calling them by name.

45. In Meiri's own opinion (*loc. cit.*, 264), a wife who refuses to see to household tasks should be "held to account regarding them according to the approach that we explained." This appears to refer back to that list–as a unit–of exaggerated restatements of the language of several authorities, including Maimonides.

46. *Mishnei Torah, Chovel u-Mazzik*, chaps. 2-5.

47. For an extended discussion of this analogy with source texts, see my *Ketubah Kit for Rabbis* (eBookShuk.com, 2003), Appendix A, "What is Marriage?"

48. From the classic sources and Maimonides, it's not clear whether exercising this option also exempts her from the home-based management responsibilities; later authorities were divided on this question.

49. *Supporting evidence*: When the talmudic rabbis later formulated parallel statements to the Mishnah, they conversed in Aramaic, a cognate language in which first-person and third-person participle inflections do differ. Those talmudic formulations used a first-person plural verb form that unambiguously implies "we."

50. *Kofin* comes from the root *k-f-h*. (*Kofin* is its plural participle, implying present continuous–that is, normative–action.) The root appears in the Bible only once, as an inflection of the same verb, where the context suggests "tone down, suppress, subdue" (Prov. 21:14). (On the Bible's relevance to Maimonides' audience for understanding the meaning of Hebrew words, see Goitein, *op. cit.*, II:205-7; V:429-30.) In rabbinic literature, the exemplar of the figurative legal usage is Tosefta *Ketubot* 5:5, where this same verb (in the singular!) is applied reciprocally to both wife and husband–and thus clearly not in the sense of applying physical force: "A husband shall not insist (*eyn . . . kofeh*) that his wife nurse his friend's child; and a wife shall not insist (*eyn . . . kofah*) that her husband [agree] that she may nurse her friend's child." (The husband's interest in nursing decisions arises from the legal requirement that he pay his nursing wife a higher salary.)

Nine hundred years later, Rav Sherira Gaon's responsum (note 22) used the Aramaic cognate to *kofeh*–again in the singular, with the husband as its subject. But the Gaon went on to discuss what happens if the husband "petitions the court to ban her"; if the husband really had the power to act on his own, such court intervention would have been superfluous. Thus, the Gaon employed our verb as a trope.

51. On why a range of options is warranted–and not spelled out–see section 5 and note 24. Remedies need to be flexible also on purely economic grounds. A particular wife's obligation to work depends on local custom (§ 21.1) and her wealth (§§ 21.6-7); meanwhile, what her husband is paying her in salary and benefits depends upon *his* wealth (§§ 12.10-11).

52. Its root means "to swing, be light, move to and fro." In the Bible, the noun form is rare; concrete usages appear only in 1 Kings 12:11, 14; Nahum 3:2; and Proverbs 26:3.

53. The term also appears in a tale wherein the Angel of Death brandishes *shota de-nura* (Aramaic: the fiery switch) to induce a reluctant rabbi to give up the ghost (*Moed Katan* 28a, end). And in a few playful settings, the Talmud uses the Aramaic cognate *shotita*, understood by Rashi as a branch of the myrtle shrub.

54. See Maimonides' similar paraphrase at *Gerushin* §§2.20. Cf. Talmud of Babylonia,§*Yevamot* 106a, where the court's *kofin oto* is distinguished from *al korcho* (against [the husband's] will).

55. Other authorities roughly contemporaneous to Maimonides preserved "switch" as a trope (vs. words). See Isaac b. Abba Mari of Marseilles, *Responsa of the Provençal Sages* I:84, p. 315; Tosafot *Ketubot* 70a s.v. *yotzi*; and RaMBaN, *Kiddushin* 13b s.v. *ve-od de-Rav*.

56. In § 15.7, Maimonides surely uses the term *shot* only because of its direct tie to the Talmud, in lieu of the more usual term *makkat mardut*, which is actual flogging with the same intent. See also note 59. The term *shot* appears only twice more in the *Mishnei Torah*, in *Talmud Torah* § 2.2 and *Melakhim* § 3.8. As in *Ishut* § 15.7, both contexts make clear that a literal switch is meant and that the purpose is to induce cooperation, and the verb "strike" is used.

57. Cf. *Mishnei Torah, Rotzeiach* § 2.14; *Sanhedrin* § 16.8-9. The terms' prior connotations are:

(1) *retzua* (strap [of leather]) connotes judicial flogging, for it is the term classically used to describe it in rabbinic literature; see Mishnah *Makkot* 3:12-13.

(2) *chevel* (rope) connotes judicial flogging, for it is the means by which punitive flogging in Maimonides' day was actually administered (*teshuvah* of Hai Gaon [c. 1000], *Toratan shel Rishonim* II, p. 41; as adduced by S. Assaf, *Ha-Oneshin Acharei Chatimat ha-Talmud*, p. 55).

(3) *shevet* (rod) connotes the exertion of authority in a household, for it alludes to the biblical passage where a master strikes a slave (Exod. 21:20-21); see also Talmud of Babylonia, *Horayot* 11b.

(4) *pizra* (stick; this Aramaic word lacks a direct Hebrew cognate; Rashi rendered it as *makkel*) connotes a husband's taking the law into his own hands, for it alludes to the classic expression for "judicial self-help" (Talmud of Babylonia, *Bava Kamma* 28a; *Bava Batra* 99b; cf. Tosafot *Ketubot* 62b s.v. "Rav Huna," end).

58. Based on Talmud of Babylonia, *Ketubot* 86a-b. To be distinguished from punishment for a crime already committed.

59. So far as I know, in halakhic literature the term *makkat mardut* is never applied to a refusing wife. Disciplinary flogging is, however, prescribed for a husband who refuses to divorce his wife when obliged by law to do so (*Gerushin* § 2.20; see the explanation there). By his use of different language there and in *Ishut* § 15.7 versus the wording in § 21.10a, Maimonides invites us to ponder the essential difference between the divorce-refusing husband and the work-refusing wife. My own answer is that in the former case, physical coercion can improve the situation; in the latter case, it can only make things worse.

60. Rabinovitch (*op. cit.*, 449) asserts that *kofin ot-ah . . . ve-shot* is grounded in the court's exigency jurisdiction (*Sanhedrin* § 24.9). This is wrong. As generally in the Mishnei Torah, Maimonides deals here with regular law; a wife who refuses to work is not per se an exceptional case that requires invoking emergency powers to maintain social order!

61. Consider especially the mutually corresponding rights, duties, and constraints on the will of each party–structurally balancing the interests of one party against the other–that add up to portray marriage as a partnership based in reciprocity (see, for example, §§ 12.1-4, 13.14, 15.19-20).

62. *Kofin* cannot possibly refer to the husband, yet the wife is its object in § 15.15; the context is clearly the court. Likewise in § 21.17; the couple is divorced, so clearly the husband no longer has any authority over her. Cf. § 12.11 and § 15.7, where the husband is the object of *kofin*, yet nobody suggests that Maimonides gives a wife the right to hit her husband. (Also, identify places in the *Mishnei Torah* or in rabbinic literature where *kofin* is used to refer clearly to only one of the parties to a dispute.)

63. Compare § 21.10a to the only other appearance of *kofin . . . ve-shot* in the *Mishnei Torah*, where Maimonides adds the verb *makkin* ("hit, strike, beat"). See the end of Excursus 2.

64. Various commentators, such as RaBaD, *Migdal Oz*, and *Marei Mekomot* (Brooklyn: Kehot, 1984), have explicitly sought sources but to no avail. True, Meir Havazelet (op. cit.) pointed to a passage in the late 14th-century commentary by Rabbenu Nissim (RaN) on Alfasi's *Ketubot* 63b, s.v. "Rabbi Yosé." The passage begins, "When she says, 'I will not do [work],' *kofeh ot-ah ve-shutim*"; and it concludes, "so said the 'gaon' (*ve-khakh omer ha-gaon*)." Havazelet claimed that this was Maimonides' Gaonic source for allowing a husband to hit his wife. But from analyzing the passage's literary structure and the legal history of its components, it becomes clear that like his predecessor Ibn Adret (note 37), Nissim was cataloguing the approaches put forward by various Rishonim; thus, "so said the *gaon*" must refer only to the last of the several options listed (which is known to be the opinion of Ibn Migash, Sherira Gaon, and perhaps Hai Gaon as well; see notes 21 and 22). "Gaon" cannot refer back to the start of the catalogue (which, ironically, is surely a restatement of Maimonides' words, not their source). In his 1958 edition of *Mishnei Torah*, R. Samuel Tanhum Rubenstein made the same mistake as Havazelet, albeit more subtly; *Sefer Nashim*, p. 170, n. 40. Grossman (2001), although identifying the *gaon* as Hai, otherwise repeated the misreading of Nissim's passage, pp. 380, 385; so did Dorff (2003), p. 289, n. 14.

Working in the Orthodox Jewish Community

Rabbi Dovid Weinberger

SUMMARY. This article is based on a presentation made at The First International Conference on Domestic Abuse in the Jewish Community–*Pursuing Truth, Justice and Righteousness: A Call to Action*, sponsored by Jewish Women International and Partners, held in July, 2003, in Baltimore, MD, USA.

This presentation was part of a workshop moderated by Nechama Wolfson, Executive Director, Shalom Task Force. *[Article copies available for a fee from The Haworth Document Delivery Service: 1-800-HAWORTH. E-mail address: <docdelivery@haworthpress.com> Website: <http://www. HaworthPress.com> © 2004 by The Haworth Press, Inc. All rights reserved.]*

KEYWORDS. Abuse, Orthodox Jewish community, Jewish law, role of rabbis

My purpose today is to give you a little bit of an insight into some of the laws that are coded in what we know as the *Shulchan Aruch*, the Code of Jewish Law. It deals very sensitively with three areas in particular: physical abuse, emotional abuse, and sexual abuse. These laws are scattered, in many, many different places throughout the Code of Jewish Law, and in lot of the rabbinic literature. It's for that reason, that there are many rabbis who aren't so acquainted with these laws. Part of what we do

[Haworth co-indexing entry note]: "Working in the Orthodox Jewish Community." Weinberger, Rabbi Dovid. Co-published simultaneously in *Journal of Religion & Abuse* (The Haworth Pastoral Press, an imprint of The Haworth Press, Inc.) Vol. 6, No. 3/4, 2004, pp. 75-82; and: *Domestic Abuse and the Jewish Community: Perspectives from the First International Conference* (ed: Rabbi Cindy Enger, and Diane Gardsbane) The Haworth Pastoral Press, an imprint of The Haworth Press, Inc., 2004, pp. 75-82. Single or multiple copies of this article are available for a fee from The Haworth Document Delivery Service [1-800-HAWORTH, 9:00 a.m. - 5:00 p.m. (EST). E-mail address: docdelivery@haworthpress.com].

in rabbinic training in certain cities is to gather the rabbinic leaders, and have a conference. My part, generally, is to delineate to them some of the sources where we see the sensitivity of our Torah, of our source of all Jewish law, and how the Jewish woman is held in such high regard.

I want to begin with a Talmudic sentence, a Talmudic statement, which tells us that, forever, which means always, "a person should be careful with the honor of his wife." "There is no blessing in the home, any good, anything that's valuable in the Jewish home, only comes about because of the Jewish woman." So therefore, we are told, "Be very careful with the honor of your wife, of your spouse." Then there's a corollary statement of the rabbis. It tells us you are to love your wife, your spouse, as yourself, you are to give her and accord her honor even more than what you would expect or want for yourself. So right at the source, at the bedrock and at the base of all Jewish teaching is the great honor that the rabbis have put on the Jewish woman. I say this very, very emphatically at the beginning, because unfortunately, many people out there have a different vision. I'm talking about the general public, and perhaps even within our own communities. People have a very skewed and blurred vision of what the Torah outlook is in terms of honor that is to be accorded to one's spouse, and specifically to the Jewish woman.

As I go through some of the sources, I'm just giving you a little snippet in the amount of time that I have to delineate some of these views in rabbinic literature. After that I'd like to speak about the role of rabbis in the community which is crucial and critical in any community in order to be able to do the work that Shalom Task Force does or for that matter, really, any valuable work in the community–it has to involve rabbinic leadership.

Let me begin to just discuss a little bit about physical violence in the Code of Jewish Law. I'm going to delete the sources just for the sake of brevity, but know that they're here. Anybody who would want them I will make them available to you. But the *Shulchan Aruch*, the Code of Jewish Law, states very clearly that a man who beats his wife, who hits his wife, commits a great sin. And if he's accustomed to doing this, meaning it wasn't the happenstance occurrence that it happened once accidentally, but it seems to be a pattern, a recurring pattern, then the Jewish court of that community has the ability to excommunicate the person. There are different forms of how this is done. I'm not going to go into the details of excommunication. Has it been done? Yes, it has been done. Should it be done more often? Perhaps yes. But the reality is, it goes in stages. It doesn't come immediately–excommunication. In rabbinic sources, it speaks about the progression. Of course, first the person is spoken to, to see if he understands that this is a sin, it's sinful, it's wrong, and it cannot be done. It's not to be tolerated. It's not sanctioned. Jewish law does not permit this. This is sinful. If he's willing to say, "Yes, I realize that. I can't help myself. Help me." Okay, then we work with the person. We don't excommunicate such a person. We say, "Look, you want to be helped. We'll help you. There are sources that we can send you to. There are professionals that deal with this problem. And you'll get helped." But if a person is not interested, and he's not forthcoming, or he's just somehow willing to stand firm and resolute against any rabbinic figure that he believes that he can go up against . . . then the rabbis have permission even to physically restrain such a person, whatever that might take. Finally, as I say, to excommunicate.

Now, people have a notion that men, because they hold a card to the *"get,"* which is the Jewish bill of divorce, and they have to give it, that somehow the women are helpless. The rabbis will say, "Well, if your husband doesn't want to divorce you, even though we understand your plight and it's very difficult and you're being abused, whether physically, emotionally, sexually, whatever or combinations of abuse, but unfortunately, you know, we have to wait for him to be willing to give it." So that's another untruth, and that's really a misconception. Because there are certain cases in Jewish law where we force, and we are permitted to force, the husband to give that *"get."* So that we don't have to wait for him to come on his own laurels and say, "Okay, I think I'm ready now." No, no, no. We can force the circumstance. One of those situations, very clearly stated in the Code of Jewish Law: if he doesn't listen to the words of the *beis din,* of the Jewish court, in terms of desisting his activity, ceasing and desisting. We force him to divorce. And a woman may in many such instances come forward to the rabbi initially, perhaps of her own synagogue or a rabbi in the community and say, "These and these are the situations." And I want this to be documented, which there's a lot to be said about, which is not really the purview of my discussion today. But documentation of course is crucial and critical, so that everything is written down. It's presented. That woman can then go to a rabbinic court and say, "These are the facts. This is the way it is. I insist on a divorce." Yes, the rabbis have the right to force it. Will they force it? Again, it depends how well-informed they are. Who's advocating on her behalf? And there's a lot that goes into that.

Another statement of the rabbis that's crucial is that a woman, as opposed to her husband, is given, what we call in Jewish terms *"keskas kashrut."* That means, the word kosher you're all familiar with. Usually we think of it in terms of food. But it means that the person is kosher. It means we sanctify in terms of solidifying the statement as being correct and valid, that of the woman as opposed to the husband. We don't have witnesses. We have nobody there. There are no hidden cameras in their house, in their bedroom. We don't know. The husband has one story. The wife has another story. Maybe she drags him to the rabbi. Now, who's telling the truth. Is she right? Is he right? Who did this, who started, who provoked, who then continued. It's really immaterial. It really is irrelevant. Facts here are irrelevant. Because rabbinic literature teaches us clearly, emphatically that the woman is given total and complete veracity in terms of what she says. And for good reason. Clearly maybe she was generally viewed as the weaker of the two, and that the husband would take more of a forceful and dominant role that would lead to this. Because it's clearly a very high percentage only one way [husband abusing the wife]. Men can be abused, but we know the reality, that it's a very, very small percentage. Overwhelmingly it's always the abused woman. The rabbis therefore have said that when the woman makes a statement, "I've been abused," it's taken as fact. It's not to be questioned. And it's not to be countered. So in the Code of Jewish Law, it's very clear what needs to be done.

Further on the rabbinic literature there is reference to situations not only of physical violence but of what we would call emotional violence. Emotional violence is name-calling, and it's being put down or it's restricting one's wife in terms of doing certain activities. So the rabbis, for instance, tell us in relationship to issues with in-laws: The husband might say, "You are not to go to your parents' house. I insist. I forbid you for going because your mother is this, your father is that, and I got into a fight with them, or I don't like them." The husband has no right. That's abuse. That's considered abuse. That's not just family domestic issues. That's abusive. He might never lay his hands on her, but that's considered abuse. He's holding her back. He's restraining her in a different way. Once again, rabbinic leadership is to get involved. They are to take steps to stop this, to the point, if necessary, of forcing the *"get,"* as we said earlier.

Then we have another area, which is sexual abuse. Here again the sensitivity of our rabbis is unbelievable in terms of the honor and respect that is to be accorded the Jewish woman. For that matter really any human. I shouldn't keep stressing the Jewish woman. Because Torah law speaks about honor and respect for humans, for the human being, and the honor that has to be given to them. But now we're talking about Jewish law. So I'm specifically speaking about the Jewish woman in this regard. There are religious rights that come with marriage. In the document of marriage known as the *"ketubah,"* it speaks about the fact that the husband has marital obligations besides financial obligations to his wife, and he also has certain rights in that regard. But there definitely comes a fine line when it's crossing the line and it's considered abuse. Where the woman perhaps finds the husband to be despicable due to his activities or due to other situations of his lifestyle, and she doesn't want to be with him. And she refuses to go to a *"mikveh,"* a ritual bath, in order to become spiritually cleansed so that she can be with him. Very often a husband will state that, "You are a rebellious wife." There's a Jewish law which is known as a *"moredes." "Moredes"* means a rebellious wife who refuses to do what she's to do as a wife. Part of the job, so to speak, of a woman is certain activities in the house: taking care of the house and the children and so on, and being there for the husband in certain ways. If all of a sudden she just abrogates that responsibility and runs away, so we would say, you know, you're rebellious. If you're rebellious, you're not entitled to anything. So if you run away, I'm not going to care for you. I don't have to pay you a penny, even if you have to take up residence somewhere else. They'll threaten their wives in this way. The wife becomes scared. She's nervous. Then if she ever needs a divorce, they're going to throw this up and say, "You're not getting a divorce because you didn't follow your responsibility."

Yes, those are laws in Judaism, and they are codified in Jewish law. However, a woman who leaves with a very clear alibi, and a very reasonable one, that she would normally tell her rabbi or another rabbi in the community as to why she has to depart because she cannot live, as the rabbis call it, "you can't live with the snake in the same pit." Very often it's because of fear of the physical, and sometimes it's not because of that. It's just, "I can't. I can't come home and be belittled in front of my children, or even just between myself and my husband. I'm made to be non-existent. I can't live like this. It's not normal life." Again, the rabbis have a statement that *chayah ishis*, married life is for living, not for pain and suffering. So if you're living in pain and suffering, in any form or fashion, that's not life. That's not Jewish life. That's not what married life is all about. So such a woman would get in many instances rabbinic sanction to disappear, to a shelter, to her family, wherever it may be and in so doing, she is not considered a *moredeh*. She is not considered a rebellious wife. Again documentation is critical. It's important in order to ascertain that she got rabbinic permission to leave and so forth.

The key ingredient is that sometimes it's just simply out of a sexual element where the husband is abusing his wife. He says, "Look, I want you now, and I want you now, and this, and that, and regardless." The husband sometimes uses Jewish law to his advantage. She might not be as knowledgeable. But factually speaking, a woman is not the husband's slave in any form or fashion, especially not in this area. Therefore the wife, unless she's treated with the greatest respect and admiration, is not obligated to live with her husband according to Jewish law. If she cannot handle it because he will force her or, so to speak, rape her in a way, then she can go to a rabbi, a *beis din* and perhaps even disappear and not be deemed a rebellious wife.

Of course, in the interim, wherever she decides to go—whether she's in a shelter, whether she takes an apartment elsewhere in hiding, whether she lives by a relative somewhere—the husband's financial responsibility remains the same. Any time a wife has to depart and has to leave the marital home for reasons that are not her doing but because of an oppressor, namely in this case the husband, then she has total entitlements for all financial obligations. She needs clothing, she needs food. Her children—if she took her children with her to protect them—then they have to be paid for as well. Not always will she get that right away. But the woman has even rights to take out monies from the accounts and keep records and documentation of what she spends. Even in the event she didn't, and her family gave her the money, in the court of Jewish law, when it comes down to the final divorce, part of the settlement will be that whatever monies she's expended in order to secure her safety would be financially the obligation of the husband to repay. These are just some of the areas that deal with abuse and how the *Shulchan Aruch*, the Code of Jewish Law, and rabbinic literature look at it.

I want to spend the last few minutes on the role of the rabbi. As I said earlier, in every community there are rabbinic leaders. Certain times people have a greater relationship, a closer relationship with the rabbi of the synagogue. Whether Orthodox, Reform, Conservative, it really makes no difference. But he's a rabbinic figure, someone to turn to, somebody we would hope would have leadership quality and know what to do, and be there to assist and to help. Whether your person goes to a synagogue once a year for Rosh Hashana, Yom Kippur, and that's it, or they come every Shabbat, or they have as they say a close or distant relationship, know that a rabbinic figure in the community is crucial. If we're talking about Jewish law and how the process will emerge and how to continue, you don't want to do things on your own.

You want to do things with a rabbinic stamp. Because then you're safer. You're better off. You know that you have somebody who knows your plight, knows your situation. Should it be necessary down the line in a court of Jewish law, there's somebody who can testify that everything that you did was done with his approval every step of the way. That's extremely crucial.

But in addition to that, if we're looking at the broader picture, and there are, violence cases everywhere. So if I talk to rabbis in California or in Denver or Miami, wherever I speak to colleagues of mine, some are more understanding of it. Some are a little bit more advanced in the process. Others are getting there. But we're all aware that it's out there. Those that are more open will probably get more cases. Those that seem to be removed from things are probably not going to get that many people coming to them. So it's important to educate the rabbis in the community. As I said, one of the things we do is rabbinic training. We gather them together in the community and we give them a little bit of an understanding of the rabbinic law that's involved.

But critical is that the rabbis work together within a community. There are communities that are closer knit, and there are those that are much more widespread. Every community has its own dynamic. But what is important is one simple fact. That's something that I believe each of you in your own community can accomplish right away. If we're talking about domestic violence, you have to bring all the rabbis together. Here's where we take off our hats and we don't really make a difference who we are, what we are. We have to work together to save the Jewish family. That's the concept here. Jewish children and the Jewish woman. So we're talking about what we call in Hebrew *pikuach nefesh*: lifesaving work. Lifesaving work. Forget about who I am, who you are, who your congregants are, who my congregants are. You have to bring them all together and say, "Look, we have one common goal. Sickness? Illness? We're all together. Lifesaving issues of the Jewish family, we all have to be together." Because there really are no differences. We have to save them. We don't need tragedies, which unfortunately have befallen our people in many, many communities because people were ignorant. People gave the wrong advice. They said, "Go back. He'll be good. This or this or this." Unfortunately, a funeral took place shortly after that. We can ill afford even one such circumstance. Therefore, it's necessary that you deal with your rabbi and the other person in the community that you get a hold of, the other rabbi, and say, "Look, let's get together. We have to deal with this as a community." If you have a batterer, an abuser in your synagogue, and he's going to come to mine, that's not going to be a safe haven for him. Because this rabbi and that rabbi and the third and the fifth and the eighth we're all on the same page. He's not going to be allowed into any synagogue unless he goes for help, unless we can bring him to the next step. That's crucial. That's something that Jewish women can accomplish. You have to stand strong and firm together, to bring all the rabbis in the community as one, and as I said to realize that this is a life and death situation.

HEALING AND WHOLENESS

Community Culture:
Community Response

Marcia Cohn Spiegel

SUMMARY. The *hasidic* movement of the 18th and 19th century was one in which male teachers and wise men taught boys and men in a sex segregated environment. In the late 20th century a spiritual movement of Jewish renewal began that is now called *neohasidism*. Open to both men and women, its leaders are charismatic teachers and *rebbes*. Some individuals drawn to this community seek healing from past abuse, or spiritual malaise and may be vulnerable to abuse by leaders who cross sexual boundaries. Policies and procedures are suggested for protecting the safety and integrity of participants, while maintaining the open, loving atmosphere for learning and prayer.[1] *[Article copies available for a fee from The Haworth Document Delivery Service: 1-800-HAWORTH. E-mail address: <docdelivery@haworthpress.com> Website: <http://www.HaworthPress.com> © 2004 by The Haworth Press, Inc. All rights reserved.]*

[Haworth co-indexing entry note]: "Community Culture: Community Response." Spiegel, Marcia Cohn. Co-published simultaneously in *Journal of Religion & Abuse* (The Haworth Pastoral Press, an imprint of The Haworth Press, Inc.) Vol. 6, No. 3/4, 2004, pp. 83-92; and: *Domestic Abuse and the Jewish Community: Perspectives from the First International Conference* (ed: Rabbi Cindy Enger, and Diane Gardsbane) The Haworth Pastoral Press, an imprint of The Haworth Press, Inc., 2004, pp. 83-92. Single or multiple copies of this article are available for a fee from The Haworth Document Delivery Service [1-800-HAWORTH, 9:00 a.m. - 5:00 p.m. (EST). E-mail address: docdelivery@haworthpress.com].

KEYWORDS. Sexual abuse, charismatic leaders, neohasidism, Jewish renewal

I was asked to speak about how the *neohasidic* movement has dealt with sexual abuse by charismatic leaders, a subject on which I am passionate. I wavered between relating horror stories of women and girls, boys and young men who have been abused or presenting dry information on organizational policies and procedures. While preparing my remarks I had a call that reminded me that this is an issue that is alive in this community of spiritual seekers, and we cannot pretend it does not exist, nor can we protect, deny and make excuses for the perpetrators of such abuse.

My expertise in this field is not as a scholar, but rather as someone to whom victims trust their stories. In the 25 years since I started speaking publicly about my work with alcoholism and addiction in Jewish families, I have never finished a lecture, a class, or a workshop without someone coming up to tell me their story of abuse, domestic violence, incest, or clergy sexual abuse. I have heard well over a thousand such stories and too many of them have been about Shlomo Carlebach, one of the beloved founders of this movement. Most of the stories begin, "I've never told anyone this before . . ." followed by a recitation of painful memories of exploitation and distress. It often takes years before the truth and the horror of this life experience can be confronted so that the victim can move on to become a survivor. In this paper I will not discuss the problems of pedophilia, child pornography, or sex addiction which have been widely exposed in the media in recent weeks. These behaviors cut across denominational lines. While, they are reprehensible and need to be addressed, in this paper I will focus specifically on issues that relate to this movement once called Jewish renewal, now called *neohasidism,* and suggest some policies to create a safe, comfortable place for all who choose to participate.

Because I am aware of the dangers implicit in an intense week of spiritual study and ecstatic worship, when I taught at the *Kallah,* the summer retreat of ALEPH, I often half-joking admonished the faculty to "Keep your fly zipped and take a lot of cold showers." It sometimes got a giggle, and sometimes evoked private conversations about starting a new relationship with a participant. I learned that I was not alone in my concern. Over a hundred years ago Reb Menachem Nachum told his *Hassidim* (students) to take cold baths in the house of study–or in the court of the *tzaddik* (wise man)–to inoculate them against temptation.[2]

He was describing a world where young men, some barely post pubescent, and often recently married, went to live and study with their *rebbe* (teacher) or *tzaddik* for weeks at a time. The intensity of their worship, study and living arrangements often aroused erotic feelings that needed to be addressed. The intense male fellowship carried with it a degree of homosexual innuendo, as well as an acute awareness of the convergence of sexuality and spirituality.

Reb Shaya Isenberg describes the *rebbe* as a *morei derekh*, a guide on the path, who is sometimes seen as a *Mashiach* (messiah) by his *Hassidim*. He is the one who can fix broken souls, who can heal the consciousness of others so that they can move on. It is said of this *rebbe* that he "should lead his flock, not the flock the leader; when the people turn from the path, he turns around to guide them back; the *rebbe* should not lead out of self-interest; he hooks his *Hassidim* up with the holy *shefa*, the divine flow of blessing and sustenance into the world; he opens the gates of divine blessing for the people, changing evil decrees."[3]

The *rebbe* then is a man of great power among his followers. They put their trust in him for his guidance. This is a movement of charismatic leaders and *rebbes*. *The World Book Dictionary* defines charisma as "a divine gift to a devout person conferring upon him powers of healing and prophesying." *Webster's Dictionary* expands on this definition, "it is a personal magic of leadership arousing special popular loyalty or enthusiasm for a public figure" and finally in *Roget's Thesaurus* synonyms are allure, influence, power, seductiveness. The importance of our teachers is born out in the *Mishnah* which tells us that while one's father brings one into this world, one's teacher brings one into the world to come. We give our leaders enormous power and influence over our lives.

Reb Zalman Schacter-Shalomi points out that Reb Shneur Zalman described a *tzaddik* as someone who doesn't have a shred of *yetzer hara*, (evil inclination) left. The rest of us may behave like the *tzaddik* only by great struggle to control our thoughts, words, and deeds. When we teach, lead *davenning* (prayers), or give a sermon and the chemistry is right we feel inflated. It's a wonderful feeling. However, it is important to remember that when that moment is over we are no longer the *rebbe*, or the *tzaddik*, but just another person. Reb Zalman points out that charisma will not happen without a group that elevates you to that place, with the understanding that it is a temporary position that someone else can occupy at another time to do the holy work.[4] The danger here is that even when the teacher understands the temporary nature of the role, the student may not be able to separate from that powerful charismatic moment.

The *neohasidic* movement started in the 1960s and 70s when there was an open and permissive attitude about sexual behavior. The introduction of the birth control pill encouraged freer expression of sexuality by both men and women than the one in which I grew up in the 1930s and 40s. Because of the advent of feminism in the movement we had to acknowledge that this permissiveness could sometimes have profoundly negative consequences. While the earlier *Hasidic* movement was composed only of male rabbis and their male students, this is a hands on egalitarian association. The role of the *rebbe* is still central, but now the *rebbe* can just as well be a woman as a man, the students both women and men. The confusion of the erotic and spiritual that was present for earlier *Hasidism* continues to exist, only now this is no longer a sex segregated community. I recently attended *Shabbat* services that started out quietly, moving to joyous expression and then building to ecstasy. I felt extremely uncomfortable when the energy began to move from ecstasy to eros. Worshippers in the 21st century are confronted with the same confusion that the young men felt more than a century ago.

Who are the people who are drawn to this movement? Some suffer from brokenness, a spiritual hunger, a sense that God is missing in our synagogues. Some are seeking mystical wisdom, healing, and Jewish techniques for meditation. Many years ago when I joined a 12-step program, I needed to accept a Higher Power in my life in order to take the first steps. My rabbi and other Jewish professionals to whom I turned for help assured me that there was no such concept in Judaism. (I sometimes wonder if any of them ever think about the content of the prayers they recite daily.) I struggled to pray in the synagogue I had helped to build because I felt that I was the only one there who believed in God and the efficacy of prayer. When I found Jewish renewal and worshipped with others who opened their hearts, it was like returning to a home I had never known. Over the years I have heard many stories of what drew people to *neohasidism*. For some it was a sense of a great void they were seeking to fill, a hole in their heart that needed to be repaired. For others it was a search for healing from some form of abuse in their life–physical, emotional, or sexual.

These women and men are eager to belong to a group that promises to help them move forward in their lives, to connect to God, and to be part of a community of other seekers. They are particularly vulnerable, defenseless, and can easily be harmed when someone whom they see as trustworthy and powerful crosses sexual boundaries. They may feel privileged to be singled out by their *rebbe*. They may even be the one to initiate or encourage the sexual contact. They put great faith and trust in the leader from whom they expect protection and support. Sometimes they elevate the *rebbe* to a Godlike position–almost a form of idolatry. The *rebbe* is seen as representing God, and when he perpetrates sexual abuse, they feel betrayed not only by him, but by God as well. Their faith is shaken, if not destroyed.[5] We must help our leaders as well as our followers. Reb Zalman teaches that we must enhance the sacred quality of the mutually freely chosen relationships of adults, while guarding against coercive and overpowering behavior.[6] And Reb Shaya Isenberg adds, "We need the teachings of our tradition to guide us on a moral, compassionate path in our daily interactions, and we also need to be taught how to tune into our inner sources of moral guidance.[7]

I started by saying that I had a call recently that reminded me of the urgency of confronting these boundary issues. It came from a young woman who had been abused by a man she trusted many years ago, a teacher and a friend. A long time has passed since her experience, but the abuse she suffered continues to pain her. She wrote to me about her feelings: "As an orthodox woman, there is a tremendous amount of shame for women related to any premarital sexual involvement, and a girl is likely to be humiliated into silence, as I was. He was particularly powerful in laying on the shame factor. He actually told me that it's a woman's fault if a man is uncontrollably attracted to her, and made me really afraid to tell anyone–and thus shame myself. I physically fought him (tried to keep him from touching me), but was too afraid to call for help. Unfortunately, he was much more physically powerful than I was. It's hard to imagine now, but I was really brainwashed by this man. It took me years to emerge from the confusion of what he told me and understand that I was a victim. I can imagine that other young women may be too confused about their experiences to speak out." She is struggling with how to confront her continuing pain and to reclaim her sense of power and personhood.

In the past if a woman came forward to tell her story of being abused, she often met with disbelief.[8] The community wanted to protect the reputation of a loved, and revered leader. She was accused of exaggerating; misunderstanding his exuberant affection; or of spreading unfounded gossip, *la shan hara*. She may have been so shamed that she left the community. At the very least she became even more vulnerable and confused. The Torah grapples with this dilemma: is she a liar, or is she warning us of real danger? We are told in Leviticus 19:16 "Thou shalt not go up and down as a talebearer among thy people; neither shalt thou stand idly by the blood of thy neighbor." While our sages teach that gossip is akin to murder, they also tell us that we must rebuke those who are doing wrong. In *Bereshit Rabbah* (54:3) Reb Yosi bar Reb Hanina teaches: "Love unaccompanied by *tochecha*, rebuke, is not love." In the *Mishneh Torah*, Law of Ethics, (6:7 & 8) Maimonides tells us that we should first rebuke the wrongdoer in private, in a way that does not shame him. However if he does not repent than he should be shamed in public, reviled and his sin declared. In our litigious society how do we deal with the accusation? Is it enough to stop inviting the perpetrator to participate in our programs and activities or do we need to warn others in order to protect them?

In an article entitled, "Can justice and compassion embrace?" Rabbi Drorah O'Donnell Setel is concerned that both of the individuals, the perpetrator and his/her victim, are cared for. Those who have been abused grieve the fact that there wasn't a purpose to their suffering. As a community we need to say to them that while there wasn't a *reason* for their suffering, there can be a *purpose* to it, to make sure that this suffering doesn't happen to others. On the other hand, she says, "You can't write off all the valuable and meaningful things someone has done because he is a perpetrator of abuse . . . We have a responsibility as a larger community to provide advocacy and healing for the work they need to do as well as the victim." She goes on to say, "The advocates for the victim have to hold that victim in their hearts as a human being . . . with a soul, and perpetrators also deserve someone who holds them in their heart. BUT IT CAN'T BE THE SAME PEOPLE." The victim must be made to feel safe and supported and the perpetrator helped to do real *tshuvah*, to take responsibility for his actions, feel remorse and change his behavior. If we don't demand accountability we are ignoring the problem and allowing the perpetrator to cause harm to other individuals in the future.[9]

ALEPH, the renewal community, is concerned with creating an environment where each participant feels safe and respected. Their code of ethics states that "when we create intense spiritual community we are opening the door to opportunities both for great holiness and great danger. There is a thin line between spiritual energy and libido–the psychic space where one is open to ecstatic experience can also be a space where one is open to manipulation and exploitation." The code goes on to state that faculty and leaders have a "responsibility to make sure that every participant is present and grounded at the end of any class or group experience." That events are structured "so that powerful group energies are guided by competent and experienced leaders who respect and guard the boundaries of every participant."

Teachers, service leaders, or persons in any position of authority at an ALEPH event are advised to refrain from entering into a sexual relationship with any student or participant in their program. Single teachers who meet someone with whom there is a mutual attraction are advised to wait until the event is over, to end the student/teacher or rabbi/congregant relationship, and to start anew after a suitable waiting period. The policy relies on prevention to create an environment where abuses are less likely to happen and makes it clear that anyone who feels uncomfortable is welcome to bring that concern to staff, board members, or spiritual leaders who will listen in confidence, take them seriously and respond in a way that is truly healing and supports every person involved in staying in community in a way that is safe and healthy.[10]

Mutual consent to sexual activity cannot take place without free choice, full knowledge and equal power, with an absence of coercion or fear. According to Reverend Marie Fortune, founder of FaithTrust Institute (formerly the Center for the Prevention of Sexual and Domestic Violence), if there is any imbalance of power in a relationship these factors will not be present. A *rebbe* cannot be a teacher/counselor and a lover/partner with the same person at the same time. This dual relationship will result in conflicts of expectations and interests. The member will be deprived of a safe place to seek counsel and support. If the *rebbe* responds to a sexual overture by a member, then he has allowed the boundaries to be broken. It is his responsibility to maintain the boundaries. (I have heard Rev. Fortune remind clergy of their responsibility saying, "You are always responsible. It is never O.K.") The *rebbe* needs to clarify ethical standards, understand the nature of power and authority; learn how to maintain boundaries in relationships; and learn how to care for their own emotional and sexual needs in appropriate ways. They need to consult with professional peers to avoid isolation in their roles. The members must also be educated about standards and procedures.[11]

The Interfaith Sexual Trauma Institute recommends that an organization develops written standards of sexual ethics for both professionals and members, spelling out the expectations of behavior for the whole community. It should be distributed to the entire community, and renewed and signed annually by the leadership. Agreement to the conditions should be required for service. The clergy must accept full responsibility for relationships, conduct them with adequate measures including regular supervision, and taking whatever safeguards are necessary to protect themselves and their community. The policy should include procedures for reporting allegations, follow-up processes, support for the victim and family as well as for the community. Ongoing education of both professionals and members can promote sound affirming understanding of sexuality and the ability to assist members who seek help in the development of sexual and spiritual health. This policy needs to spell out how the offender will be removed in order to protect the members from further abuse, and identify him even if he leaves the community.[12] Ohalah, The Association for Jewish Renewal has developed just such an instrument.[13]

According to Reverend Fortune, we do justice by telling the truth, acknowledging the violation, offering compassion to alleviate the suffering, protect the vulnerable, hold the perpetrator accountable and offer restitution and vindication for the survivor.[14]

In addition to the requirements we make of our leaders we also need to develop educated followers. Debra Cash describes "a new ethic of followership that is skeptical and openhearted at the same time, one which retains the locus of decisions and responsibility for those decisions in each follower's measured reason and passionate feelings. A followership that honors expertise and courage and inspiration, but does not presume that a person's expertise, or wisdom in one area means that he or she is an expert or role model across the board . . ."[15]

Bob Freedman offers a different way of *rebbe*-ing. "The model of leader as servant implies a teacher/facilitator who is observant, sensitive to the character and knowledge level of the group, non-judgmental, and possessed of techniques that will enable people with a variety of different learning styles to gather information both through interaction and personal revelation. Diligent practice of mindfulness would enable such a person to be compassionate and capable of both acceptance and outreach."[16]

I think we agree that we want to create an environment that provides each participant with a sense of safety and security in a space that allows each of us to learn and grow, to worship and exult together. For years we have accepted certain group norms without a thought. For instance, we are great huggers, we embrace each other in prayer, arms around each other's waists, and I, for one, find great joy in that. But there are those amongst us whose experience of physical violation is such that they don't want to be hugged or touched, even by friends, but particularly not by strangers. How do we accommodate their need for comfort without making them feel that they are not included in our community?

We have lived with a lot of assumptions about who we are and now we need to examine our assumptions and consider their implications. We have learned that some of our beloved leaders abuse their positions; we have also learned that adult members who appear strong and independent may in fact be powerless and vulnerable. We need to help maintain their dignity and integrity, and treat them justly and with compassion.

This is not a movement with a central address or authority. It is a group of loosely connected organizations, each with different members who come with different standards and expectations. It has been a long time since the first gatherings of the *neohasidic* movement, and now it is time for us to learn from past mistakes, to set them right, and to go forward as more mature organizations.

In *Kiddushin* 40b: Reb El'azar in the name of Reb Shimon says: "Because the world is judged by the majority of its deeds and an individual is judged by the majority of his/her deeds, an individual who does one good deed should be happy, because s/he has tipped the scales meritoriously for her/himself and for the world. Woe unto the individual who commits one transgression, because s/he has tipped the scales deleteriously for her/himself and for the world." We remember that it is not our duty to complete the task, but it is our responsibility to begin.

NOTES

1. The following paper was presented on a panel, "The Role of the *Rebbe*: Leadership and Ethics in Contemporary Neohasidism." at *Awakening, Yearning and Renewal: A Conference on the Hassidic Roots of Contemporary Jewish Spiritual Expression*, at the Jewish Community Center in Manhattan, NY, March 28, 2003. Thanks to those who helped me: Janet Carnay, Rabbi Cindy Enger, Susan Saxe, and Rabbi Sheila Weinberg.

2. Biale, David, *Eros and the Jews: from Biblical Israel to Contemporary America*, Basic Books, a division of Harper-Collins, 1992. p. 130.

3. Isenberg, R. Shaya, "The Rabbi as Transpersonal Moreh Derek," *New Menorah: The Journal of Aleph: Alliance for Jewish Renewal*, No. 47, Spring, 5757, 1997: pp 1+.

4. Schacter-Shalomi, R. Zalman, "Notes toward a field of Rebbetude," *New Menorah: The Journal of Aleph: Alliance for Jewish Renewal*, No. 46, Winter 5757 1996: pp. 1+.

5. Fortune, Marie M., *Is Nothing Sacred? The story of a pastor, the women he sexually abused, and the congregation he nearly destroyed*, Harper San Francisco, 1989.

6. Schachter-Shalomi, Zalman M., "The Renewal of Jewish Renewal," *New Menorah: The Journal of Aleph: Alliance for Jewish Renewal*, No. 42. Winter 5756 1995 p. 1.

7. Ibid.

8. Blustein, Sarah, "Rabbi Shlomo Carlebach's Shaddow Side," *Lilith*, 23:1, Spring 1998, pp. 10-17.

9. Setel, Drorah O'Donnell, "Can Justice and Compassion Embrace?" Diane Gardsbane editor, *Embracing Justice: A resource guide for rabbis on domestic abuse*, Washington, DC, Jewish Women International, 2002, pp. 52-58.

10. Gabriel, Cindy and Susan Saxe, "A Space Where Everyone Belongs," *New Menorah: The Journal of Aleph: Alliance for Jewish Renewal*, No. 64, Summer 5761, 2001: pp. 1+.

11. Fortune, Marie M., *Is Nothing Sacred? The story of a pastor, the women he sexually abused, and the congregation he nearly destroyed*, Harper-San Francisco, 1989, p. 106.

12. Interfaith Sexual Trauma Institute, *Guidelines for Written Standards of Sexual Ethics in Ministry* and *Recommendations for the Prevention of Clergy Sexual Misconduct*, www.csbsju.edu/isti

13. OHALAH: Association of Rabbis for Jewish Renewal, P. O. Box 631, Daly City, CA 94015.

14. Fortune, Marie M., *Is Nothing Sacred? The story of a pastor, the women he sexually abused, and the congregation he nearly destroyed*, Harper-San Francisco, 1989, pp. 114-117.

15. Cash, Debra, "Followership" *New Menorah: The Journal of Aleph: Alliance for Jewish Renewal*, No. 46, Winter 5757 1996: p. 7.

16. Freedman, Bob, "Take Over from Within: A Model for Rabbi-ing," *New Menorah: The Journal of Aleph: Alliance for Jewish Renewal*, No. 46, Winter 5757 1996: p. 8.

Renewal and Reconciliation
After Family Violence?

Gus Kaufman, Jr.

SUMMARY. This article is based on a presentation by Dr. Kaufman at a workshop with Laura Davis and Rabbi Drorah Setel. The author notes that without their contributions this discussion is incomplete. The workshop description read: How and why do men who batter change? Should reconciliation between survivors and former perpetrators be a goal? How should Jewish institutions respond to the questions? What Jewish texts and traditions can we draw upon to consider these issues? The author addresses the first question: How and why do men who batter change? *[Article copies available for a fee from The Haworth Document Delivery Service: 1-800-HAWORTH. E-mail address: <docdelivery@haworthpress.com> Website: <http://www.HaworthPress.com> © 2004 by The Haworth Press, Inc. All rights reserved.]*

KEYWORDS. Domestic violence, justice, social change, renewal, reconciliation

Over twenty years of working with men who have battered their partners have led me to identify four reasons men batter: it works, they can get away with it, they learned to, and trauma re-enactment. I will touch

[Haworth co-indexing entry note]: "Renewal and Reconciliation After Family Violence?" Kaufman, Gus Jr. Co-published simultaneously in *Journal of Religion & Abuse* (The Haworth Pastoral Press, an imprint of The Haworth Press, Inc.) Vol. 6, No. 3/4, 2004, pp. 93-100; and: *Domestic Abuse and the Jewish Community: Perspectives from the First International Conference* (ed: Rabbi Cindy Enger, and Diane Gardsbane) The Haworth Pastoral Press, an imprint of The Haworth Press, Inc., 2004, pp. 93-100. Single or multiple copies of this article are available for a fee from The Haworth Document Delivery Service [1-800-HAWORTH, 9:00 a.m. - 5:00 p.m. (EST). E-mail address: docdelivery@haworthpress.com].

Digital Object Identifier: 10.1300/J154v06n03_09

on these in more depth, but for now I want to consider the implications of this information for questions of renewal and reconciliation after family violence. *For men to stop battering it has to not work, men must not be able to get away with it, we must learn differently, and we must successfully address the creation, prevention, and healing of trauma.* This last imperative means we must forget punishment–the repetition of violence (cf. James Gilligan, *Preventing Violence*, 2001.) But these imperatives also mean men must be held accountable for their abusive behavior–there must be consequences. This is both an individual and a collective necessity. Collectively we have much to do to build our society, our synagogues, our families into places where violence doesn't work, men can't get away with it and power and control aren't ways of organizing relationships.

What does this process of *teshuvah* (turning, repentance) look like? Individually, men must:

1. Stop battering. This means learning what battering is. While men learn the behaviors and attitudes of male supremacy, dominance, and centrality growing up, we do not learn to see this from the perspective of the oppressed. In fact, much of learning to "be a man" is learning to dis-identify, to objectify, to not feel.

2. Own what we've done. This accountability is paradoxically more likely to start in a setting with other men who called to be accountable–the very setting those who abuse most avoid. Our social instincts are to privatize abuse and dealing with abuse. The first book on battering was entitled *Scream Quietly or the Neighbors Will Hear*. At a recent meeting of people seeking to organize synagogue responses to domestic violence the participants, many abuse survivors, agreed that these issues would most likely be brought to the rabbi, if anyone, not to others in the synagogue. Yet I question how effective a rabbi alone can be in getting a man to stop his abuse. My experience is that groups of men have the power and can model for other men really owning and taking responsibility for what they have done. In the batterers' program I co-founded, each orientation session for men considering entering the program included a man who had been through the course telling the story of what his abusive behavior had been and how it had affected his partner, children, and others. This statement had been written and rewritten as he learned, through confrontation, with support, to own more and more honestly and completely his actions and their effects.

3. Listen–this means learning how to listen and being willing to listen. I have come to believe the quintessential batterers' statement is "Shut your g-damned mouth!" Battering is fundamentally an attempt to obliterate the other as an actor/speaker. Listening means appreciating the other's reality, autonomy, and enfranchisement. In our batterers intervention classes we taught men not to interrupt. And then to let go of "white-knuckle listening," in which we prepare a rebuttal as the other is talking. Respectful listening also means not contacting her if and when she doesn't want to be contacted. To learn about the effects of his behavior and stance, a man has to listen to the woman he has attempted to silence and other women. We had men read battered women's books and watch their videos and movies. (We can't intimidate a book). Men need to hear in synagogue and from the bimah from women also. And see women listened to and respected by other men there.

4. Make restitution and work for justice. Pay child support, do our share of childcare, alimony, therapy costs, etc. Don't force her from the synagogue. No longer support the silencing and suppression of women and their interests. A man who went through a batterers' program at Brother to Brother in Rhode Island quotes a statement "only when a batterer permanently forsakes all control over his partner does he cease to be a batterer. Few achieve this." Anne Ganley, a psychologist who pioneered batterer intervention groups, sheds light on why that is in her chapter in *Feminist Approaches for Men in Family Therapy*, when she speaks of "men's socialization to the concept of entitlement in relationships with women or family members." Ganley states that "In order to better meet their intimacy needs, men need resocialization to accept 'no's' from women and family members, to experience disappointment rather than anger at those times, and to perceive these 'no's' as being acts of autonomy rather than as acts of attack on them" (p.17).

5. Heal. Learn about ourselves, learn other ways to relate, practice them, own and heal our wounds. Connect with others in non-controlling intimate ways. Give and get support from other men: don't expect women to do all the emotional/relational work–(connecting us to our families and others.) Trauma involves numbing: Carol Gilligan has said men learn to be "specialists in disconnection." Paul Kivel and the Oakland Men's Project have called this the "Act Like A Man" box. (Cf. *Men's Work* and *Boys Will Be Men*.) An earlier formulation of this, which I helped revise for the

manual *Men Stopping Violence: A Program for Change*, is called the "male emotional funnel system." Instead of learning to show no emotion or anger used to control others, we men must learn to identify, acknowledge and express the whole spectrum of feelings. To do this we must confront homophobia/sexism–the idea that emotional vulnerability and caring are feminine and therefore inferior or taboo. Judaism has offered us the idea of maximizing the *yetzer hatov* (the impulse toward good) and transforming the *yetzer hara* (evil impulse); this is good but not specific enough. From Pesso Boyden System Psychomotor therapy, a body-based system of emotional re-education and healing (see *http://www.pbsp.com/*) I have taken the idea that we each have the developmental tasks of integrating our masculinity and our femininity, our power and our vulnerability. PBSP has also taught me a powerful technology for understanding the specific phenomenology of trauma/abuse and of recovery, an area that has continued to grow since Judith Herman's groundbreaking book, *Trauma and Recovery.*

All these efforts are necessary to set the stage for the possibility of renewal and reconciliation. We have in mainstream society almost no images of men taking responsibility for abusive actions and doing the hard long work of *teshuvah*. This is not a sudden conversion, but a process. In searching for models of men changing, and of the change process, I remembered Alice Walker's great novel *The Color Purple*. In its last section we have an example of repentance and change by an abuser that's convincing. As Celie, the long-abused narrator of the story, finally escapes from Mister_____(she refuses to write his name), she says to him: "I curse you . . . until you do right by me, everything you touch will crumble . . . Until you do right by me, everything you even dream about will fail . . . Every lick you hit me you will suffer twice, I say . . . the jail you plan for me is the one in which you will rot."

She escapes. When she returns to the area much later she hears that Mr. has become "not so quick to judge . . . he clean that house just like a woman. Even cook and wash the dishes when he finish." We hear how he was suffering until he sent Celie the rest of her sister's letters, which he had withheld from her–"Meanness kills." Still later she is able to write to her sister "he work and he clean up after himself and he appreciate some of the things god was playful enough to make . . . when you talk to him now he really listen . . ."

Still later they are able to discuss Shug, the woman they both love. Mr. admits he was jealous—"I wanted to kill you and I did slap you around a couple of times." He speaks of what a fool he was. Celie:

> Well, I say, we all have to start somewhere if us want to do better, and our own self is what us have to hand.

> I'm real sorry she left you, Celie. I remember how I felt when she left me.

> Then the old devil put his arms around me and just stood there on the porch with me real quiet. Way after while I bent my stiff neck onto his shoulder. Here us is, I thought, two old fools left over from love, keeping each other company under the stars.

> Other times he want to know about my children.

More time passes and in a conversation Celie says:

> You know how long it take some mens to notice anything, I say. Took me long enough to notice you such good company, he say. And he laugh.

> He ain't Shug, but he begin to be somebody I can talk to.

In my presentation I did not address questions of what is the work for those who have been abused. Rabbi O'Donnell Setel considered what Jewish texts and tradition offer on the subject of whether *teshuvah* always involves forgiveness. Laura Davis, in her magnificent book, *I Thought We'd Never Speak Again: The Road From Estrangement to Reconciliation*, gives us many stories and maps of the possibilities. A few of the things I gleaned from her book:

- That true reconciliation requires a deep acknowledgement of the injury we have suffered.
- The five R's of *teshuvah*: recognition, remorse, repentance, restitution, and reform—stages one must go through in order to be forgiven for an offense.
- Reconciliation is ongoing. Accountability must therefore be ongoing and active also. Without accountability there is only so far reconciliation can go.

- When you continue to act violently, your pain and sorrow never go away.
- For justice we need to: (1) Make the victim whole; (2) Restore the perpetrator, so he can be a contributing member of society; (3) Achieve this with compassion and nonviolence.

It's important to give people the chance to make right what they've screwed up. Obviously, this cannot be imposed on another. For me, however, I feel a need to see perpetrators as human or risk losing some of my humanity.

My approach to renewal and reconciliation after family violence has evolved. The battered women's movement and the approach to intervention with men who had battered that grew out of it said men must be arrested, convicted and jailed. This would send the message that battering is a crime and that the perpetrators would be held accountable. Women of color in particular have criticized this approach as not adequate, because our criminal justice system is not rehabilitative. Men should not be degraded and broken down further. As I have looked deeper into my own history and that of the abusive men with whom I have worked, I have been influenced by those who have studied trauma and its transmission. I have come to believe that men who abuse learned to do so. Their traumatic histories–and what we call male socialization is in varying degrees traumatic–must be addressed. But this work may have to follow, or at least be simultaneous with, their work to be accountable for the suffering they have inflicted. Yael Danieli, editor of the *International Handbook of Multigenerational Legacies of Trauma*, in a talk at Emory University posited the following steps as necessary for healing:

- Justice is critical to healing and includes: investigation of the crime; bringing it to trial; conviction; punishment; redress; restitution
- The perpetrator officially acknowledges responsibility and remorse to the victim: acknowledgement; apology (extremely important to the victim); redress (which includes compensation, both material and symbolic); financial restitution
- Commemoration

Where there is a flight into reconciliation without these steps there is the opposite of justice and this becomes a new traumatic factor. Danieli's co-presenter, Dori Laub, of Yale University, a Holocaust survivor remarked: "it doesn't cost the perpetrator to acknowledge what happened." They quote Bruno Bettelheim: "What cannot be talked about cannot be put to rest" and so wounds fester generation to generation.

My belief is that Judaism has always acknowledged the tension of the individual and the societal. In the story of our liberation from Egypt, for example, we follow two individuals–an abuser, Pharaoh–a just man– Moses, as they make choices that both represent and affect their peoples. It is not a simple polarity–both the oppressed people and their leader will be called to account for their bad behavior at other times. This polarity is repeated again and again in the Bible–in the story of Jonah and Nineveh, the prophets, the Maccabean revolt. I mention this because just such a tension informs work to end abuse. We must think of: (1) what we can do about abusers other than ourselves and (2) what we can do about ourselves. On the one hand we have the battered women's movement–women claiming moral authority/voice–but this arose from countless individual struggles given voice. One of its powerful tools– the Power and Control wheel–came from a group of women at the Domestic Abuse Intervention Project, Duluth, MN cataloging their individual experiences. Out of women's insistence came the call and the pressure for men to begin to change. When each woman's story so resonated with others, it became clear that battering was not about individual pathology, but social control–that its true context was social norms of hierarchy. It was only when these norms were challenged, such that battering no longer worked, that batterers' intervention programs arose. Thus, when a man who has been abusive begins to work with his own *yetzer hara* involving abuse of a family member (1) he is likely to be and needs to be doing so within a structure of accountability, safety for his former victims and sanctions–societal support that helps produce (2) his decision/choice/intention to be non-abusive–which means giving up power over others, working for equality, justice, restitution = *teshuvah*. How often are all these conditions in place today?

If we want family violence to become as unthinkable as slavery and lynching are today, we must transform society, building interpersonal, familial and social practices and institutions that teach and support justice and equality and negatively sanction domination and hierarchy. We must do this in a way that is itself nonviolent, humane and just.[1]

NOTE

1. One effort in this direction is my new organization Retreat From Violence, Inc. (See *www.retreatfromviolence.com*).

REFERENCES

Danieli, Y. (1998). *International handbook of multigenerational legacies of trauma.* New York: Plenum.

Davis, L. (2003). *I thought we'd never speak again: The road from estrangement to reconciliation.* New York: Harper Collins.

Ganley, A. (1991). Feminist therapy with male clients. In M. Bograd (Ed.), *Feminist approaches for men in family therapy* (pp.1-21). New York: Harrington Park Press.

Gilligan, J. (2001). *Preventing violence.* New York: Thames and Hudson.

Herman, J.L. (1992). *Trauma and recovery: The aftermath of violence–From domestic abuse to political terror.* New York: Basic Books.

Kaufman, G., Bathrick, R. Carlin, K., and Vodde, R. (1987). *Men stopping violence: A program for change.* Atlanta: MSV, Inc.

Kivel, P. (1992) *Men's work: How to stop the violence that tears our lives apart.* New York: Ballantine Books.

Kivel, P. (1999). *Boys will be men: Raising our sons for courage, caring, and community.* Canada: New Society Publishers.

Pesso, A. www.pbsp.com, articles, Slide introduction to Pesso Boyden System Psychomotor Therapy.

Pizzey, E. (1974). *Scream quietly or the neighbors will hear.* London: Penguin.

Walker, A. (1982) *The color purple.* New York: Harcourt Brace Jovanovich.

PROMISING PRACTICES

Ayelet Program:
Mentoring Women Leaving
the Cycle of Violence

Elana Dorfman

SUMMARY. In 1998, the Haifa Battered Women's Hotline started Ayelet, a unique project, which provides long-term mentoring to women who are starting a new life outside the cycle of violence. From the studies of the shelters between 30% to as much as 60% of the women who leave their violent partners return to them within the first six months. The Ayelet project has had a 100% success rate. All the women who have participated in the project have succeeded to rehabilitate their lives and live outside the cycle of violence. Furthermore, Ayelet works to stop the generational cycle of violence. By helping the mothers leave the cycle of violence and create a new non-violent family model, their children

[Haworth co-indexing entry note]: "Ayelet Program: Mentoring Women Leaving the Cycle of Violence." Dorfman, Elana. Co-published simultaneously in *Journal of Religion & Abuse* (The Haworth Pastoral Press, an imprint of The Haworth Press, Inc.) Vol. 6, No. 3/4, 2004, pp. 101-108; and: *Domestic Abuse and the Jewish Community: Perspectives from the First International Conference* (ed: Rabbi Cindy Enger, and Diane Gardsbane) The Haworth Pastoral Press, an imprint of The Haworth Press, Inc., 2004, pp. 101-108. Single or multiple copies of this article are available for a fee from The Haworth Document Delivery Service [1-800-HAWORTH, 9:00 a.m. - 5:00 p.m. (EST). E-mail address: docdelivery@haworthpress.com].

will hopefully become free from the devastating effects of witnessing parental violence. *[Article copies available for a fee from The Haworth Document Delivery Service: 1-800-HAWORTH. E-mail address: <docdelivery@ haworthpress.com> Website: <http://www.HaworthPress.com> © 2004 by The Haworth Press, Inc. All rights reserved.]*

KEYWORDS. Haifa, Ayelet, domestic violence, Jewish community

INTRODUCTION

At the First International Conference on Domestic Abuse in the Jewish Community sponsored by Jewish Women International in Baltimore, I had the honor of presenting a model for mentoring women who leave violent relationships and start to rehabilitate their lives. This program is called in Hebrew: Ayelet Project, where the word Ayelet is both a common Israeli name for a woman and also forms an acronym meaning adoption support and accompaniment. Ayelet is a project of the Haifa Battered Women's Hotline. The project was first started as a local Haifa project in 1998 by a grant from the Haifa Municipality, which continues to support it today. In 2001 it became a national project with the help of the Matan Foundation and is currently being funded by a generous grant from the UJA Federation of New York.

The Haifa Battered Women's Hotline, a nonprofit women's volunteer organization, was founded in 1990 and its primary mission was to extend aid through telephone counseling to women in violent relationships and to raise awareness to the problem of violence against women in Israel. From the beginning, the Hotline was conceived as a Jewish Arab organization and provided culturally sensitive services in both languages. Very soon it became evident that there was a need for services in Russian and a new immigrant from the FSU joined the Hotline. Now the Hotline provides services in five languages: Hebrew, Arabic, Russian, Amharic (the Ethiopian language), and English, and does outreach to many of the diverse communities in Israel.

In 1997, when the Ministry of Labor and Social Affairs wanted to open a national hotline for victims of domestic violence, it used the Haifa Hotline as a model of good practice. Later the Ministry chose the Haifa Hotline to run the National Hotline for the Prevention of Domestic Violence and for Children at Risk. Since then the Hotline answers approximately 5,000 calls a year from all over the country through a toll free 1-800 number.

The Hotline's focus is on how to help a woman in a violent relationship. This is an extremely complex problem that involves overcoming emotional, psychological, legal, and societal barriers. The Hotline's approach is systemic and covers both aid to the individual victim, improving services, and raising awareness to create social change. The first challenge is getting exposure so that any woman suffering from violence will know the number she can call. Despite the tremendous strides that have been made in Israel towards making people aware of the extent of violence in our homes–about 1 in 5–most women still feel that if they are battered it is a private problem, they blame themselves and feel great shame. This is the first barrier to getting help. The Hotline does extensive outreach in five languages in order to change society's attitude, to clearly put the responsibility for the violence on the perpetrator and not on his victim. The hotline makes it clear that women need not be ashamed if they are battered and to empower them to seek help.

Once the woman calls the hotline the next challenge is to see her through the long psychological and often legal process that is involved in stopping the violence. When a woman calls the Hotline, more often than not, she is not ready to make any major changes. She needs reassurance that she is not the only one in this situation and she needs to begin to believe that it is possible to make a change and that there are people who can help her. Typically, after several calls the Hotline volunteer may begin to suggest options: perhaps to try therapy for herself or her husband; to take out a restraining order against him; to move in with relatives or friends for a while; to move out to her own apartment or perhaps to shelter. The Hotline can intervene on her behalf, with the police or other community services. We can provide her with legal advice or refer her to a social worker in her neighborhood or to a shelter. Besides a few follow-up calls the relationship with the Hotline usually ended if a woman made a change and either moved out or got a divorce or went into a shelter.

From the studies of the shelters between 30% to as much as 60% of the women who leave their violent partners return to him within the first six months. Many of the women despair from the pressures of poverty and loneliness causing them to give in to their violent partner when he promises, once again, to change. This then was the next challenge of the Hotline: how to help these women successfully rehabilitate their lives and not return to the cycle of violence. This was the impetus to create the Ayelet project.

THE NEED

The first six months after leaving a violent relationship are the most difficult. The women who are starting over are usually in a new city away from their families without a network of support. They may be in the midst of looking for a new job, running to numerous court sessions, and dealing with the anger and frustrations of their children who have been uprooted from their home, school, and friends. In addition, many of the women suffer from Post-Traumatic Stress Disorder (PTSD).

Violence trauma brings the victim to a face-to-face confrontation with human evil. The longer the violence continues the more twisted the psyche of the victim as she desperately tries to survive in an inhuman situation. PTSD has recognizable symptoms including over stimulation, flash backs, disassociation, fatigue, and a limited ability to interact with one's environment.[1] Many women leaving the cycle of violence are confronted with anger, resentment, and shame from their surroundings. Society often blames them as if they were responsible for the bringing on the violence or that it is their fault that they didn't leave. This is why many battered women experience, distancing, hostility, abandonment, and isolation, which increase their need for help. Victims of violence can suffer from PTSD for as long as a year after the trauma and some for as long as their lives. Therefore they need long-term aid and support.

When a woman is battered she is not the only victim in the family. In a paper published by the Minerva Institute for Youth Studies, Professor Zvi Eisikovits states that there is a positive correlation between children living in violence-ridden family environments and their impaired development in the physical, cognitive, emotional, behavioral, and social domains. Children exposed to parental violence have trouble forming friendships among their peers and the stressful, often terrifying, situation at home drains their energies to such an extent that they cannot concentrate on their studies. Sons, who are exposed to their fathers beating their mothers, when they grow up, have a 1000% higher rate of wife abuse than sons who are not witnesses.[2] Without intervention these children may grow up greatly disadvantaged in all areas of life and form the core for continuing violence in the generations to come.

The Ayelet project addresses both these problems. If a woman chooses to leave a violent relationship, she will have the personal and community support she needs to succeed at rehabilitating her life. Furthermore, Ayelet works to stop the generational cycle of violence. By helping the mothers leave the cycle of violence and create a new non-violent family model, their children will hopefully become free from the devastating effects of witnessing parental violence.

HOW DOES AYELET WORK?

An abusive partner is a controlling partner in which violence is only one of the ways that he exerts his control. Another way is to keep her financially dependent on him for all her needs. He may also isolate the woman from any network of support or potential aid. The violent husband will disapprove of any female friends the woman may have and routinely pick fights with her family. After years of abuse a woman finds herself lacking not only economic resources but also the self-confidence she so desperately needs to sustain the transition. In addition, she is often completely isolated socially.

Research into mentor relationships between women and adolescent girls shows that those girls who had a mentor who listened, understood, and validated their experiences and feelings evidenced transformations in personal confidence and ability.[3] We have found that adult women respond just as positively to the mentoring relationship. Despite the many great pressures facing a survivor of violence, often including severe poverty, it has been our experience that it is enough to break the isolation in order to help a woman successfully start over.

The Ayelet project has had a 100% success rate. All the women who have participated in the project have succeeded to rehabilitate their lives and live outside the cycle of violence

The Ayelet project pairs a trained volunteer mentor to each survivor of domestic violence in the program. The volunteer meets with the woman approximately once a week and may accompany her to the court, social worker, the bank, she may help her with bureaucratic hurdles, or just spend time with her, listening to her, and offering emotional support.

Rena (fictitious name) ran away from her violent husband 5 times before finally divorcing him. She was referred to the Hotline from the shelter and when she came to Haifa she participated in the program. Hannah Ramot, an Ayelet mentor, was assigned to accompany Rena. During that time Hannah was her main support. When Rena was ill with a high fever, her 10-year-old daughter, not knowing where to turn, called Hannah for help. It was Hannah, not Rena's family, that called the ambulance and sat at her bedside in the Hospital. Hanna took Rena's daughter home until a suitable arrangement could be made during

Rena's ten-day stay in the Hospital. During the two years that Hannah mentored Rena, she helped her to find a job first as a cook for an old-age home and then later, helped her to open her own after-school daycare in her home.

Rena is just one of the 50 women who have been helped by the Ayelet program. Often the road to independence and economic self-sufficiency is long and painful. Rena has told me that without the constant encouragement and emotional support that she received from the program she doesn't know how she could have accomplished what she has in the last two years.

Ayelet volunteers participate in a four-month training course. The course operates on two levels. On one level the volunteers learn about domestic violence, post-traumatic stress disorder, community services that are available, legal issues, and some job counseling skills as well. On another level the volunteers participate in group sessions where they share stories of their own experiences of trauma and how they dealt with those experiences. The have the opportunity to get in touch with their own feelings of despair and hope and prepare themselves emotionally to be able to mentor a woman coming out of a violent relationship.

Upon completing the course, the volunteer is assigned a woman to mentor. She will accompany her from six months to a year and sometimes even longer. This is very important since as was mentioned earlier many of these women suffer from PTSD and therefore need long term support. Community help, such as social workers, are not trained to recognize the symptoms of PTSD and cannot possibly accompany a woman for the long term. Furthermore, the women suffering from years of abuse by a controlling husband have lost the ability to take control of their lives. Any authority figure such as a social worker only increases her dependency. A volunteer, on the other hand, approaches the women from an equal footing, woman to woman and therefore helps her to regain control over her life.

The mentors receive group supervision twice a month in order to sustain them emotionally in their difficult task. These supervision meetings for a support group for the mentor where she can exchange practical information as well as improve her mentoring skills.

GOING NATIONAL

The Hotline has always extended services beyond telephone crisis intervention including outreach, legal aid and short-term accompaniment to women leaving the cycle of violence. In 1998, the Hotline started the Ayelet Project which provides long term accompaniment to women in Haifa who are starting a new life outside the cycle of violence. Upon becoming a National Hotline we became aware of how important it was to provide these services locally in other areas of the country. It is our aim to use the Hotline's expertise and years of experience to set up volunteer centers in other parts of the country to provide these services. The volunteers who weekly answer the crisis phone lines are acutely aware of the need for these centers so that any women in the country can receive the same help that the Hotline can extend in Haifa.

In 2002, Ayelet plans to set up new volunteer centers in different parts of the country. These centers will provide short-term accompaniment to women leaving the cycle of violence, and mentoring to women who have left the cycle of violence. It is hoped that some of the volunteers will lecture and run workshops to raise awareness to prevent domestic violence and that the centers will recruit volunteers who can give aid in Hebrew, Russian, Amharic, and Arabic.

The Hotline will train volunteer coordinators and work in cooperation with existing organizations that already provide services, in Jerusalem, Beer Sheva, Tel Aviv area, and Acre. In addition, the Hotline is training volunteers in Daliat el Carmel and Tamra, two Arab towns in the north of Israel.

CONCLUSION

The Ayelet project is innovative and creative; it has a long-lasting impact on the women it serves since it empowers them to change their life. Recently the Hotline received a letter of thanks from a woman who first called the Hotline three years ago and was part of the Ayelet program. She wrote "You believed in me when I did not have the courage to believe in myself. You held up a mirror to me so that I could see myself the way you saw me. Thanks to you I began to believe that I could deal with my violent husband, deal with the bureaucracy and court system, and finally deal with making a home for my children and myself. You showed me the light at the end of the tunnel and continued to hold it up for me until I arrived there."

NOTES

1. Herman Lewis, J. (1992). *Trauma and Recovery, (9-11)*. New York: Basic Books.

2. Eisikovits, Z. (1997). *Children's experience of inter-parental violence: A heuristic model*. Minerva Center for Youth Studies.

3. Allison, T., Catherina, A., Taylor, L., Williams, M. Jordan, J. V., Miller, J.B., & Liang, B. (2002) "The Relational Health Indices: A Study of Women's Relationships." *Psychology of Women Quarterly*, 26, pp. 25-36.

Community Organizing
to Address Domestic Violence
in Immigrant Populations in the USA

Nadia Kasvin
Angela Tashayeva

SUMMARY. This article is based on a presentation made at The First International Conference on Domestic Abuse in the Jewish Community–*Pursuing Truth, Justice and Righteousness: A Call to Action*, sponsored by Jewish Women International and Partners, held in July, 2003, in Baltimore, MD, USA. *[Article copies available for a fee from The Haworth Document Delivery Service: 1-800-HAWORTH. E-mail address: <docdelivery@haworthpress.com> Website: <http://www.HaworthPress.com> © 2004 by The Haworth Press, Inc. All rights reserved.]*

KEYWORDS. Domestic violence, community organizing, immigrant populations, Jewish community

The Russian-speaking population in Columbus, Ohio is estimated at 7,000 people. About 5,000 of them are Jewish refugees and immigrants from Russia, Ukraine, Belorus, Kazakhstan, Georgia, Moldova, and

[Haworth co-indexing entry note]: "Community Organizing to Address Domestic Violence in Immigrant Populations in the USA." Kasvin, Nadia, and Angela Tashayeva. Co-published simultaneously in *Journal of Religion & Abuse* (The Haworth Pastoral Press, an imprint of The Haworth Press, Inc.) Vol. 6, No. 3/4, 2004, pp. 109-112; and: *Domestic Abuse and the Jewish Community: Perspectives from the First International Conference* (ed: Rabbi Cindy Enger, and Diane Gardsbane) The Haworth Pastoral Press, an imprint of The Haworth Press, Inc., 2004, pp. 109-112. Single or multiple copies of this article are available for a fee from The Haworth Document Delivery Service [1-800-HAWORTH, 9:00 a.m. - 5:00 p.m. (EST). E-mail address: docdelivery@haworthpress.com].

Available online at http://www.haworthpress.com/web/JORA
© 2004 by The Haworth Press, Inc. All rights reserved.
Digital Object Identifier: 10.1300/J154v06n03_11

109

Uzbekistan. Compared to other cities, Columbus has a very small Russian-speaking Jewish population.

Our agency, Jewish Family Services, started in 1908 as a response to the needs of Jewish immigrants, and it continues to be one of our core services. Up until 1996, these services were limited to initial reception, placement, and resettlement, which is provided the first 4 months in the country. Resettlement and adjustment do not end at 4 months. Even after basic needs are met, other more complex issues come up. Seven years ago we started educating our agency staff and our major funders that there are gaps in services provided to the Russian-speaking Jewish community. We started with identifying those unmet needs through surveys, focus groups, and conversations with various individuals, leaders of the community. The results of those efforts were not surprising for us, but it provided us the validation for seeking additional funds.

At the same time, several cases of domestic violence in our community were brought to our attention. We needed new services and new funds to meet these needs. Next two years we spent educating ourselves on issues of DV, researching available funding, and writing grants.

In 1999 we received our first grant from the state of Ohio; and, several months later we received a federal grant from the Office of Refugee Resettlement. The funding was for outreach, education, and direct services to victims of family violence. We were fortunate to have had time to prepare for this program and discuss some ideas on how we wanted to start to implement the program.

We could not just gather people from the community and tell them that we wanted to talk to them about family violence. They would shrug and say, "It is not about us." The program started with conversations about women's issues, women's rights, children's issues, family relationships, differences between two cultures, even though we also realized that it is not easy to bring people together for these topics of conversation.

When recruitment for the program staff person began, we were very happy when Angela Tashayeva applied. Angela already had an extensive network of her own; she was well known, respected, and trusted in the community. With a background as a teacher in Russia, she was a perfect candidate.

Our decision to hire Angela came as a huge surprise in the community. We did not even have to do any advertising about the program. People were so intrigued by a new program and Angela's responsibilities, that they called our offices, stopped Angela in a grocery store, and approached her at parties. Angela made so many small and large group presentations during the first 3 months of the project that we achieved our original goals for the first 6 months.

Additionally, we went to different parts of a city to meet with people and introduce our services for immigrants. We went to English as a Second Language (ESL) classes and citizenship classes, community meetings, Russian grocery stores, and apartment complexes with significant populations of Russian-speaking residents, including those for Russian-speaking seniors.

The education and outreach went in two directions: education of our community and education of mainstream providers. We educated our community on issues of domestic violence, and we educated mainstream providers about our community. Staff provided training for the Bar Association, Mediation Services, Children Services, Franklin County Department of Job and Family Services, etc. One of our biggest successes was a training for a local Police Department. All officers were trained on issues of domestic violence in the Jewish community and cultural sensitivity in regards to the Russian-speaking population. The response was very positive and now we maintain a close relationship with the local Police Department.

As with all the other programs represented on this panel, we also created outreach materials and brochures that were both linguistically and culturally sensitive.

A tremendous amount of work was accomplished during the first year of the project. Positive response to this effort was confirmed when Jewish Women International asked us to do a training for Jewish women, leaders in their own communities, who came to the United States from Russia and Ukraine for 10 days to learn more about domestic violence prevention programs. We held a reception and a lot of people from our community came to show their support of our efforts.

We had to be very creative to be able to encourage women to attend presentations and meetings. We identified issues *they* were interested in and started to introduce issues of family violence, little by little, at each meeting until women felt comfortable talking about abuse and violence.

Also, it was very important to have meetings on a regular basis. When meetings were not scheduled during the summer, several women called and told me that they missed those meetings. This is how Women's Club started. We invited women who have been in the United States for five, ten, fifteen years, and those who just came several months ago. Women were able to share their experiences and help each other. The more they learned about the family violence, the more comfortable they became helping victims of violence in our community.

Some members of the Women's Club admitted that they were victims themselves. More women called and began coming to us for help.

After a year of working on the project, there was a new challenge: how to keep women interested? To respond to this challenge:

- Events were organized bringing women and children together.
- We collaborated with our local ballet to get free tickets to performances. We distributed these tickets to active participants of our Women's Club and asked them to come 1 hour earlier for group discussions.
- When a Russian-speaking rabbi came to town, we collaborated with him on putting together events for our community and introduced a topic of creating family traditions and rituals.
- We collaborated with a local company to do self-defense training for women and teenagers.
- When we come back from the conference, we are going out with members of the Women's Club to a Russian restaurant to share our experiences at the conference.

We will continue to come up with new ideas and encourage you to share with us any ideas that you may have.

Domestic Violence
in the South African Jewish Community:
A Model for Service Delivery

Brenda Solarsh
Jane Frankel

SUMMARY. This paper provides an overview of the response to domestic violence in the South African Jewish community, specifically that provided by Jewish Community Services, Johannesburg. The context is briefly presented in terms of the major challenges facing the South African community, the Jewish community *per se*, the impact of apartheid, the post-apartheid era, specifically the significance of crime, violence, and emigration. Brief reference is made to domestic violence within the general population. An in-depth review is given of the development of the domestic violence programme in the Jewish community, including a critical assessment of challenges and constraints to be addressed. *[Article copies available for a fee from The Haworth Document Delivery Service: 1-800-HAWORTH. E-mail address: <docdelivery@haworthpress.com> Website: <http://www.HaworthPress.com> © 2004 by The Haworth Press, Inc. All rights reserved.]*

KEYWORDS. South Africa, Jewish, domestic violence

[Haworth co-indexing entry note]: "Domestic Violence in the South African Jewish Community: A Model for Service Delivery." Solarsh, Brenda, and Jane Frankel. Co-published simultaneously in *Journal of Religion & Abuse* (The Haworth Pastoral Press, an imprint of The Haworth Press, Inc.) Vol. 6, No. 3/4, 2004, pp. 113-128; and: *Domestic Abuse and the Jewish Community: Perspectives from the First International Conference* (ed: Rabbi Cindy Enger, and Diane Gardsbane) The Haworth Pastoral Press, an imprint of The Haworth Press, Inc., 2004, pp. 113-128. Single or multiple copies of this article are available for a fee from The Haworth Document Delivery Service [1-800-HAWORTH, 9:00 a.m. - 5:00 p.m. (EST). E-mail address: docdelivery@haworthpress.com].

Available online at http://www.haworthpress.com/web/JORA
© 2004 by The Haworth Press, Inc. All rights reserved.
Digital Object Identifier: 10.1300/J154v06n03_12

INTRODUCTION

Domestic violence in the South African Jewish community shares many similarities with other Jewish communities. The context, however, is specific and impacts on the way community members organize services and respond to them. This paper therefore focuses upon:

1. the context in which South African Jews live and work–South Africa today; the South African Jewish community; South African Jewish social services, domestic violence in South Africa;
2. domestic violence in the South African Jewish Community and the Shalom Bayit Project;
3. measuring effectiveness.

THE CONTEXT IN WHICH WE LIVE AND WORK

South Africa Today

We all know that we live in a global village. However, we as South Africans have lived through the dreadful days of apartheid, the rather frightening but exciting dismantling of this era and the often-traumatic transitional period, which continues. This has been a very specific experience, which shapes the way we live, think, and work.

Today we all live in an African led democracy and both benefit from the liberation of the country and suffer from the impact of the past. Poverty on a wide scale, violent crime, changing standards of health, education, and welfare services, a poor criminal justice system, and a weakened Rand have been the consequences to be faced by all. The AIDS pandemic infects millions and affects all.

However, there are many wonderful features of life in South Africa. It is rich in natural resources and has one of the finest democratic constitutions, is a model of reconciliation through negotiation, and the diversity of cultures makes it a country filled with vibrance. It has given many of us a home, an education, and continues to offer a very good quality of life for many.

The South African Jewish Community

There is a common perception that the South African Jewish community is vulnerable and is in decline. Whilst it has undergone significant change in particularly the post apartheid era it is still a thriving community. Most of South Africa's Jews originate from Lithuania. It is estimated that there are currently between 80 and 85 thousand Jews in South Africa. This is significantly down from its peak of 118 thousand in the early 1970s. The declining numbers are due to emigration, firstly as a protest against living within apartheid, and then as a result of the violence and insecurity in post apartheid South Africa. South African Jews now constitute less than .2% of the total population of 43 million people. *(13)* Over 40% of South African Jewish emigrants have gone to Australia, 20% to USA, 15% to Israel, 10% to UK/Canada, and 15% to New Zealand et al. The community has shifted to the major cities: Johannesburg–55,000, Cape Town–18,000, Durban–2,700, Pretoria–1500. *(13)*

The community always has had, and continues to have, an extremely well organized infrastructure. It has a comprehensive range of welfare, educational, religious, political and Zionist organizations. Despite decreased numbers, the community is experiencing an upsurge–a "golden age" in terms of Jewish commitment and involvement. Examples include: an intermarriage rate well under 10%, strong support for Israel, intensive religious identification, over 80% of Jewish children attend Jewish day schools, in Johannesburg there is a wide range of religious day schools including those for the Haredi community. *(1,13,14)*

There is a low level of anti-semitism in post apartheid South Africa; there continues to be a significant impact to the community linked to the Middle East conflict, the South African ANC government has a pronounced pro-Palestinian bias, but the ANC also reiterates Israel's right to exist within secure boundaries. *(14,16)* It is hoped that despite the high levels of crime and resulting insecurity, the fact that there is clear growth of a democratic culture in South Africa, a commendable constitution, implementation of sound fiscal policies and grounds for optimism in the country, that this will assist South African Jews to remain in the South Africa.

South African Jewish Social Services

South African Jewish Social Services is seen as comprehensive, enjoys a high level of financial support and is held in high esteem. The major service provider based in Johannesburg is the Jewish Helping Hand Society (JHHS), which provides a continuum of social services, for people of all ages. It offers both community based and residential care services and has a deep commitment to meeting the needs of the community in an effective manner.

The Jewish community must rely almost entirely on its own resources to fund its social services. The Johannesburg Jewish Helping Hand Society has a budget of 75 million Rand. They receive less than 5% of this budget in government subsidies. However, there have been subsidy cutbacks, particularly to homes for aged people. This is important to understood as the SA welfare or social development system has to redress the imbalances caused by apartheid, prioritise the needs of the poor, and address the AIDS pandemic.

Jewish Community Services is the division of the Johannesburg Jewish Helping Hand Society, which incorporates the Shalom Bayit Project. The professional work of the project is funded primarily by the Johannesburg Jewish Helping Hand Society.

A major challenge to the social service sector has been the significant impact of emigration–sponsorship has decreased–many high earners and those in the very productive years of their lives have left and there are many people left without family supports. The community has responded very effectively to its current challenges by developing community support systems. There has also been vigorous and effective fund raising and streamlining of services.

Domestic Violence in South Africa

South Africa has a population of over 43 million people, of whom 53% are women. There is an extremely high incidence of domestic violence and rape in South Africa. The Jewish community does not conform to these statistics. (15) Explanations for this high incidence includes increased reporting practices. Some, however, hold that "violence against women reflects the general culture of violence which is endemic in South Africa and which normalizes violence and affirms its role as a conflict resolution tactic." (15)

The official government reaction to domestic violence has been to acknowledge the seriousness of the problem. Since 1994, it has been acknowledged at the highest levels of government, evidenced in many speeches, policy statements, strategies, and legislation. In addition, there are many innovative and effective services for abused women and their children provided by the NGO sector. They tend to operate within a feminist perspective and are gradually including men in their programmes of action. Moreover, an increasingly vociferous response has been seen in the media regarding lenient sentencing of abusers. Yet, change has been detected, as was evidenced recently in Johannesburg, with more appropriate sentencing occurring.

Women's experience of abuse generally reflects global similarities. The types of abuse experienced, characteristics of abusers, and responses to service providers all reflect global similarities. The experience in South Africa differs on certain levels. For example, women living in rural areas had less access to services. Police services tend not to recognize emotional abuse and see domestic violence as trivial or a "private/domestic matter." It is probable that South African characteristics reflect third world or developing countries to a greater extent.

DOMESTIC VIOLENCE IN THE SOUTH AFRICAN JEWISH COMMUNITY

Initial Concerns About Domestic Violence

The first formal acknowledgement of Jewish Domestic Violence in South Africa occurred in 1994 in Johannesburg. The issue was raised by a guest speaker from Israel, who said, "If you don't look, you won't see it." The South African Jewish community had never looked for it . . . *(17)*. The concern about domestic violence in the Jewish Community was then raised by the Jewish Women's Organisations.

Fact Finding

In starting to identify women in abusive situations, the social workers at Jewish Community Services in Johannesburg were challenged by the hidden nature of the problem, and found a relatively low incidence of domestic violence on their case-loads.

> In the early days of this work, much criticism, sceptism, and disbelief was expressed by community members. Leaders in the community were reluctant to support a public examination of what was seen as a shame, scandal, and *"unlikely to be much of a problem in the Jewish community." (17)*

It took perseverance and courage on the part of the initial founders of the Project to continue with the work.

Exposing the Problem

The direction for dealing with domestic violence in South Africa was based on the described experiences in Israel and America, which stated that once the problem of domestic violence was highlighted for Jewish women, they would increasingly seek assistance.

It was with this premise in mind that the Shalom Bayit programme was formulated and the first seminar on Jewish Domestic Violence was held in Johannesburg in October 1994. At every presentation, women have approached the facilitators with stories of their own abuse or friends who have been abused.

The Shalom Bayit Project

The Shalom Bayit Project, which was established in 1994, is a partnership between Jewish Community Services and the Co-ordinating Council of National Jewish Women's organisations. The women's organisations incorporate a broad range of religious affiliations, the Women's Zionist organisation and the Union of Jewish Women. This is a sound combination of community representation and service provision.

Objectives of the Project:

The objectives of the project are:

- To minimize or eliminate domestic violence in the community
- To provide assistance to survivors and children
- To intervene with perpetrators of abuse
- To educate the community
- To train professionals and religious leaders about the signs and symptoms of abuse
- To lobby on behalf of those who are affected by domestic violence

Programmes

Education

Lectures and symposiums on the realities of domestic violence have been organized and well attended by members of the Jewish public. Articles describing situations of domestic violence regularly appear in the

Jewish Press. Rabbonim and Rebbetzins receive thorough training in identifying the potential signs and symptoms of an abusive relationship and the referral procedure to Jewish Community Services.

A typical training course for professionals includes:

- Gender awareness and how this can impact on domestic violence;
- The different types of domestic violence,
- Why women stay in abusive relationships,
- Indicators of abuse,
- Skills for dealing with a woman in an abusive situation,
- Risk assessments,
- The development of safety plans,
- The counsellor's personal experiences of dealing with abuse. *(18)*

Another area of training is the training of marriage preparation counsellors in detecting the signs of domestic violence. Jewish Community Services operates a well-established and very well utilized Marriage Preparation Programme. A high percentage of couples marrying in Johannesburg are obliged to participate in this programme.

Counselling

Counselling is offered to women at all stages of managing abusive relationships. An eclectic counselling approach which is heavily influenced by the work of Leonore Walker is used. The focus centres around the attainment of safety and reclaiming of personal power.

Abusers are not seen in joint counselling with the woman, as this is regarded as being contrary to her needs and may be dangerous for her. They are either seen by colleagues in the organization or referred to specialized services or practitioners. Networking with colleagues such as Rabbis, private practitioners and lawyers is frequently done.

One of the more notable experiences of counsellors has been the length and intensity of the work done regarding 'recovery.'

Group Support

The content of a typical support group includes:

- To assist the group members to better understand the abuser
- The cycle of abuse
- The effects of power and control in an abusive relationship

- A better understanding of the skills required for conflict management
- An opportunity to explore their own survival and recovery
- Exploring and building positive relationships with their children *(12)*

The Shalom Bayit Shelter

The Shalom Bayit Shelter was established in 1994. The shelter is a fully furnished apartment with a kosher kitchen and can accommodate two women and their children. The aim of the shelter is to provide short-term respite care for the women in a secret location.The shelter has not been well utilized. Possible reasons for this could be that the women in the community prefer to move in with another family member or a friend rather than the shelter.

Services Beyond Johannesburg

As was noted previously, the major concentration of Jews are found in the cities of Johannesburg and Cape Town. A group in Cape Town established a Jewish Women's Resource Centre, which is aimed at offering empowering opportunities to women. They also have a counselling arm and refer women in abusive situations to this service. The other centres have not established specialized abuse services.

MEASURING EFFECTIVENESS

Continuous monitoring of the programme has assisted the Shalom Bayit project to recognise and acknowledge which programmes have been effective, in what future directions the project should progress and which of the programmes need adjustment and enrichment.

We are going to present our perception of our effectiveness by using the model employed at Jewish Community Services. We will look at:

- Our objectives
- Identify what has been achieved and what has not
- Identify constraints
- Set future goals

What Has Been Achieved?

To Minimise or Eliminate Domestic Violence in the Community

The growth in public understanding of the problem and women making increased use of services indicates that women are acting to end the abuse more than previously, and are recognizing their right to do so. The incidence of domestic violence in the community has not been measured so one cannot assess whether it has been reduced.

To Provide Assistance to Survivors and Children

Therapeutic services to survivors and children have improved quantitatively and qualitatively. Regular measurement of individual and group counselling occurs. Evaluations have been very positive. The extent to which women use Jewish Community Services' services has increased.

To Intervene with Perpetrators of Abuse

Several perpetrators are seen at Jewish Community Services, and others are referred to specialists.

To Educate the Community

A great deal has been achieved. Hundreds of women have participated in large and more intimate workshops, and pamphlets, posters, and media articles are wide-spread. It does however appear that young people in the community do not appear to be very aware of the signs and symptoms of abusive relationships.

To Train Professionals and Religious Leaders About the Signs and Symptoms of Abuse

Ongoing qualitative training has taken place of professionals and Rabbonim, Rebbetzins, and Teachers. Notable inroads have been made. Prior to 1994, if a social worker were to have discussed a case of domestic violence with a Rabbi, she would have most probably been met with resistance and anger. Today, there is much more acknowledgement of domestic violence–Rabbi's are providing a valuable and reliable referral source to Jewish Community Services.

To Lobby on Behalf of Those Who Are Affected by Domestic Violence

A fair amount of public action has taken place, mostly in terms of media exposure

Constraints, Choices, Challenges

Denial

The issue of ignorance and denial continues to be a significant challenge and constraint. It is assumed that there are many women suffering in abusive situations who do not recognize that they are abused, or are too scared to come forward and ask for assistance. Many have been so affected by the abuse that they feel unable to act to end the situation, or believe that they are guilty of provoking the abuse. The need to dispel the myths about abuse and defeat the denial continues.

Knowledge of Incidence

There has not been local research thus far. Statistics have been extrapolated from studies done in the USA. To this end we are very pleased that a research fund has just been established by the Shalom Bayit Committee. The Judith Harrisberg Memorial Fund will support research in the field of Jewish domestic violence in South Africa.

Generic or Specialized?

One of the first challenges that the project faced during its inception is whether it should become a specialist service, or whether it should become part of the generic services offered at Jewish Community Services. The challenge of funding services has led to a culture of rationalization rather than establishing new and autonomous organisations.

Therefore, the decision to incorporate the Shalom Bayit project as one of the programmes at Jewish Community Services was a pragmatic one and the programme became one of many offered by the organisation. This has value in that the larger organisation is well known in the community and enjoys credibility and support. Nevertheless, it has been debated that perhaps more women would come forward if the service was independent. This issue remains a challenge.

Gender Issues

There is pervading patriarchy in the South African and Jewish community, which is fertile ground for the existence and flourishing of domestic violence.

It does not appear as if the majority of Jewish women in South Africa have paid much attention to the issue of gender discrimination within their own community. There have been small pockets of action and some notable Jewish women in important positions within the community. However, the leadership of Jewish community structures and organisations remains largely male dominated.

This situation requires a much more concerted programme of action. Many Jewish women are disinterested and unaware of the power relationships they confront and probably only become aware of these when they experience blocks in their professional, business or personal relationships. Feminism in the Jewish community is still fairly low key and remains an area that requires the attention of those concerned about domestic violence.

Discourses

The discourse that keeps domestic violence alive is an ongoing challenge to the project. The belief that Jewish men are not abusive, that women provoke or deserve the abuse, that women must enjoy abuse to stay, that abuse only occurs in certain of the religious communities, that exposing it encourages it, are all myths that continually need to be challenged. There is much opportunity for work to be done with youth, on a preventive level.

Anonymity

Anonymity is a challenge that the Shalom Bayit project has had to contend with since its inception in 1994. The Jewish community is very enmeshed and it has been an obstacle that Jewish Community Services has had to acknowledge in all its services. Jewish Community Services maintains strict confidentiality regarding all counselling that is offered, but it is possible that women will seek assistance from private practitioners outside of the community where they are less likely to be identified.

Although anonymity is often cited as a reason preventing women from exposing their abusive experience, it is also possible that this diminishes as she gains confidence in the service, the process and herself.

Emigration

A significant challenge is the threat and reality of emigration facing the Jewish community in South Africa. This has proved to be a disruptive feature in the Shalom Bayit project. Many of the previous co-ordinators of the project and professionals dealing with domestic violence have emigrated. This has impacted on the continuity of programmes offered by the Shalom Bayit project and has also necessitated regular training of staff in this field. The building of knowledge through writing up of materials is a constructive response to the loss of trained professionals

Future Goals:

Maintenance of Current Programme

- Awareness raising of community members—media and seminars
- Individual and group counselling
- Training for Rabbis and Rebbetzins
- Training of professionals—social workers, psychologists

New Pogrammes

- A skills development programme for women
- Training for doctors
- Work with perpetrators of abuse
- Increasing awareness of gender inequalities
- Youth programmes

CONCLUSION

It was noted that domestic violence in all countries and communities share global similarities. Nevertheless, unique characteristics of the South African Jewish experience were identified. Perhaps the most striking points we made were the continuing challenge of living in post apartheid South Africa, the loss of members of the Jewish community, and the significantly powerful and effective Jewish social service infrastructure.

We are optimistic about the future both of South Africa and the Jewish community but are not naïve about the stresses we face on a daily basis. It is in fact one of the most challenging countries within which we live.

We are very appreciative of a very concerned and committed community who have provided considerable resources for our social services. We are confident that we will be supported in our ongoing work in domestic violence.

We believe that the Shalom Bayit project of Johannesburg has been an appropriate response to the unique characteristics of our community. In measuring our effectiveness we feel that we have reason to celebrate as well as the challenge of addressing many of our constraints and we look forward to learning from all of you.

Lastly we want to pay tribute to the survivors. It is with a deep sense of respect that I pay tribute to them. It is they who have taught me everything that I know about *"The Shame Borne in Silence."* (Rabbi Abraham Twerski) *(19)*

To the women who whispered–

I didn't realize I was being abused

I didn't believe this could happen to me

I thought no-one would believe me

It was only when he broke my child's wrist that I knew I had to leave . . .

Our names are Jodi, Chana, Carol, and Leah

We are 20-years-old, 30, 40, 50, and 60.

We have endured abuse at the hands of our partners–husbands or boyfriends

We have been in these relationships for 18 months to 40 years

We have ended these relationships, some of us have left and returned

We have been badly hurt–pummelled, kicked, punched, had our fingers and knuckles broken, our hair pulled out in chunks, objects forced down our throats, hands burned

We have had our stomachs kicked while we were pregnant

We have been thrown out of a moving car in front of our young children

We have been pushed out of our houses in the darkest hours of the night

We have been sworn at, cursed, constantly humiliated, threatened with the lives of our parents and children

We all want to end the abuse

and to those who asked us for:

Support and friendship from women who know what abuse feels like

To know that I am not the only Jewish abused woman in this country

People to turn to when feeling unsafe

Understanding about why our partners abuse us

Skills to find our self-esteem again

Skills to end the feelings of powerlessness

Understanding and support to enable us to leave the relationship

Skills to learn to deal with the past–some of us left the relationship some time ago

Understanding about the impact of domestic violence on our children

Skills to manage divorce

Skills to take into new relationships

How never to be a victim again

Skills to help our children now

. . . we would like to respond with the words of the famous, much loved and revered former South African President Nelson Mandela who as is well known, was incarcerated for 27 years for opposing apartheid. Upon his release he became a model of statesmanship and making peace with his past.

He said . . . *"As long as you have an iron will you can turn misfortune into advantage."*

To all those with whom we have travelled on their road to recovery, we pay tribute to your iron will and salute your survival.

REFERENCES

1. Bruk, Shirley. *The Survey of South African Jews-Highlights, Demographic Trends and The Implications for Services.* Paper presented at the Conference of South African Jewish Board of Deputies Cape Town, South Africa, 27 August 2000.

2. Evans, Patricia. *Verbal Abuse Survivors Speak Out.* Published by Bob Adams Inc, 1993. ISBN 1-55850-304-8.

3. Evans, Patricia. *The Verbally Abusive Relationship.* Published by Adams Media Corporation, 1992. ISBN 1-55850-582-2.

4. Fawcett, Featherstone, Hearn, & Toft. (Editors). *Violence and Gender Relations.* Published by SAGE Publications, 1996. ISBN 0-8039-7649-6.

5. Graetz, Naomi. *Silence is Deadly-Judaism Confronts Wife Beating.* Published by Jason Aronson Inc., 1998. ISBN 0-7657-6013-4.

6. Hearn, Jeff. *The Violences of Men.* Published by SAGE Publications, 1998. ISBN 0-8039-7940-1.

7. Horsburgh, Beverly. *Lifting the Veil of Secrecy: Domestic Violence in the Jewish Community.* Harvard's Women's Law Journal, 1995: volunteer 18.

8. Jacobs, Lynn/Dimarsky, Sherry. *Jewish Domestic Abuse: Realities and Responses.* Journal of Jewish Communal Service, Winter 1991/92.

9. Kirkwood, Catherine. *Leaving Abusive Partners.* Published by SAGE Publications, 1993. ISBN 0-8039-8686-6.

10. Morgan, Alice. *What is Narrative Therapy? An easy-to-read introduction.* Published by Dulwich Centre Publications, 2000. ISBN 0-9577-9290-5.

11. Pokroy, Janine. *Paper presented to Women's Zionist Organization seminar.* Johannesburg, South Africa, 3 September 2000.

12. Pokroy, Janine. *The Spirit of Recovery.* Support group manual Jewish Community Services, Johannesburg, South Africa, 2000.

13. Saks, David. *South Africa Jewry-A Contemporary Portrait.* Paper presented at World Jewish Congress-Policy No. 25, 2003.

14. Saks, David. *Anti-semitism Report.* Paper presented for The Institute of Contemporary Anti-semitism and Racism, Tel Aviv University, 2002.

15. Sasool, Vermaak, Pharoah, Louw, & Stavrou. *Violence Against Women-A National Survey.* Published by the Institute for Security Studies, 2002 ISBN 1-919913-20-3.

16. Shain, Mendelsohn (Editors). *Memories, Realities and Dreams. Aspects of the South African Jewish Experience.* Published by Jonathan Ball Publishers, 2000. ISBN 0-8684-2132-5.

17. Solarsh, Brenda. *Domestic violence-a Violation of Fundamental Human Rights.* Paper presented at Women's Zionist Organization Conference: Meeting the Challenge, Johannesburg, South Africa, 17 August 1999.

18. Solarsh, Hochfeld. *Domestic violence training.* Jewish Community Services, Johannesburg, South Africa, May 2003.

19. Twerski, Abraham. *The Shame Borne in Silence.* Published by Mirkov Publications, 1996. ISBN 0-9648-5081-8.

20. Whalen, Mollie. *Counselling to End Violence Against Women-A Subversive Model.* Published by SAGE Publications, 1996. ISBN 0-8039-7380-2.

Jewish Women's Aid:
Combating Domestic Violence
in the UK Community

Mildred Levison
Judith Usiskin

SUMMARY. This article is based on presentations given by the authors at The First International Conference on Domestic Abuse in the Jewish Community–*Pursing Truth, Justice and Righteousness: A Call to Action*, sponsored by Jewish Women International and Partners, held in July, 2003, in Baltimore, MD, USA. As the only representatives at the conference from the UK, the authors described wider arenas of Jewish life in the UK, and the statutory and voluntary services in which their agency developed. They reflect on some of the mistakes and triumphs encountered in the development of Jewish Women's Aid in the UK with the hope that this will be helpful for small faith communities in other places. *[Article copies available for a fee from The Haworth Document Delivery Service: 1-800-HAWORTH. E-mail address: <docdelivery@haworthpress.com> Website: <http://www.HaworthPress.com> © 2004 by The Haworth Press, Inc. All rights reserved.]*

[Haworth co-indexing entry note]: "Jewish Women's Aid: Combating Domestic Violence in the UK Community." Levison, Mildred, and Judith Usiskin. Co-published simultaneously in *Journal of Religion & Abuse* (The Haworth Pastoral Press, an imprint of The Haworth Press, Inc.) Vol. 6, No. 3/4, 2004, pp. 129-139; and: *Domestic Abuse and the Jewish Community: Perspectives from the First International Conference* (ed: Rabbi Cindy Enger, and Diane Gardsbane) The Haworth Pastoral Press, an imprint of The Haworth Press, Inc., 2004, pp. 129-139. Single or multiple copies of this article are available for a fee from The Haworth Document Delivery Service [1-800-HAWORTH, 9:00 a.m. - 5:00 p.m. (EST). E-mail address: docdelivery@haworthpress.com].

Digital Object Identitifier: 10.1300/J154v06n03_13

KEYWORDS. Jewish community in UK, domestic violence, anti-Semitism

The United Kingdom (UK) Jewish community, usually referred to as the Anglo Jewish community, presents a very different picture to that of other Jewish communities. Of course like other Jewish communities in the world, it does take on many characteristics of the 'host' society and this will be referred to later.

There are presumed to be between 296,000 and 438,000 Jews in the UK population. Research by the Institute for Jewish Policy Research (JPR) (*www.jpr.org*) points out that the varying estimates are useful for different research purposes. It depends on whether the figure is sought to estimate the provision of kosher meals-on-wheels for elderly people, or for marketing of "Jewish" material or indeed to protect from anti-Semitism. For this last purpose, which has, we feel, most bearing on the issue of domestic violence, where both emotion and prejudice are so important, the maximum estimate of 438,000 (i.e., less than 0.5% of the total population) could be considered. The estimate by JPR is based on the results of the latest census in the United Kingdom which was the first one in which questions were asked about the respondent's religion. Until these figures were explored, community researchers had to estimate the number of Jews in the population by extrapolating from the burial figures recorded by the ecclesiastical authorities and "guesstimates" from synagogue membership records. The census questions engaged the Anglo Jewish community in several heated debates, as some feared that the records could be used for political purposes and others were reluctant to define themselves in religious terms at all.

Even in London, where the majority of UK Jews live, Jews constitute only 3% of the total population and are mainly concentrated in particular areas of the capital. It is the most minor of minority groupings in the UK population resulting in practical invisibility in the wider society. Consequently, particular needs are often not recognised. We will return to look at the effects of that later.

Problems for community services have arisen because of gaps and misunderstandings between the different religious groupings. This is no doubt also a problem for other communities but it does seem that religious differences have caused more difficulty in the UK than in many other places. For example, rabbis of different denominations find it almost impossible to meet on common ground, and this has caused extra difficulties for the founders of Jewish Women's Aid (JWA) and, indeed, all the welfare services in the UK community. However, as far as grassroots initiatives are concerned, women seem to be able to cope with differences more easily than men, and JWA's experience confirms that.

Within the Jewish community, the largest grouping religiously by self-definition is Orthodox. However, many who define themselves in this way because of their synagogue affiliation may in reality have standards of practice less stringent than those adhered to by some who define themselves as Reform or Liberal. Many feel that the Masorti movement in the UK represents more truly the old Anglo Jewish tradition (known as *minhag Anglia*) i.e., "middle of the road"–a typically British stance. Masorti is halachically observant but not fundamentalist and a fairly new but growing phenomena. It attracts Jews from all the other sectors. It is allied with the Conservative movement in the USA and the Masorti movement in Israel.

To the left are the Reform and Progressive movements, which are differentiated from each other in that the Liberal/Progressive rabbis allow patrilineal descent and have recently agreed to bless interfaith marriages (though not to conduct them). Also of course there are many who would say they are "secular" but who nevertheless may have a very strong feeling of Jewish identity.

Further right on the religious spectrum are those who define themselves as "strictly Orthodox." This sector is growing very rapidly in numbers and in power. Mostly those who define themselves in this way separate to various degrees from the wider community and also from other Jews. There are certain areas of London and Manchester with a very high number of such strictly Orthodox Jews.

The suspicion and misunderstanding with which different parts of the Jewish population regard each other reflects the class system, which is still so powerful in British society. There is still a monarch and a titled aristocracy. Some of our aristocrats may not be rich. Class is not necessarily denoted by wealth. It is determined by birth and breeding and is reinforced by the education of children which, in the upper class, is almost always provided by the same historic handful of fee paying schools. The point of entry to the real aristocracy is through birth or marriage. The upper-middle class, comprised of professionals and business leaders, is in some ways as difficult to break into than the aristocracy. It is usually achieved via education or marriage to people similarly situated.

Most people in the UK are lower-middle class, many having achieved this status through education, employment or property ownership or a mixture of all three. With the virtual disappearance of heavy industry and the sell-off of social housing, the British working class has diminished to a small percentage of the population. The vast majority of people in the UK are aware of their position in the class structure and take a strange pride in where they belong. They like to look up to their betters and down on their social inferiors.

Categorisation of UK Jews is extremely difficult. The majority, however, although they may have professional status, probably would regard themselves as lower middle class. Jews have a belief that other Jewish denominations are "not quite like us." Thus, for Jewish women subjected to domestic violence, there are additional societal problems, which come from pressures to retain or improve their place within the class structure, within Jewish society and from the anti-Semitism, which is still endemic in UK society.

Before discussing the impact of anti-Semitism, we offer a brief and subjective outline of the Anglo Jewish scene. The majority of Jews in the UK originate from the big exodus from Eastern Europe between 1890 and the First World War, supplemented by further significant waves of refugees from Nazi persecution and from Arab countries. Previously, the country had been a forbidden area for Jewish settlement after the forcible expulsion in 1290 CE. There were, however, earlier settlements of Jews. From the time of Oliver Cromwell in the 1650s, Jews trickled in from the Spanish expulsion and from other countries. Those descended from these older families, who have remained Jewish and who can trace that origin, are generally very proud of that rare connection.

There are perhaps some areas in which the UK community may be more out of balance than other Diaspora communities. This is a rapidly aging community. In other words, the proportion of unsupported elderly people in our population is higher than in general. There are several reasons for this. We consider the main reasons to be:

- **Holocaust survivors.** Many survivors arrived alone and remained alone. Therefore a high proportion of them remain unsupported by families.
- **Brain drain.** A high proportion of young graduates have left the UK to settle in the USA, Canada, Australia, or in the European Community, where they see more opportunities for advancement.
- **Aliyah.** The proportion of Jews from the UK who have successfully settled in Israel is very high (estimated to be about 16,000)

and of course represents a loss from those sections of Jewish society who are more Jewishly committed.

There are also a number of younger people who have made the journey in the opposite direction. Israelis and South Africans, academics from the "New World" and those from continental and Eastern Europe of working age may alleviate these losses. It is not known what figure to put on this. Jewish immigration has impacted on the figures but more continue to leave than come in.

For North American readers, it is important to stress the close connection between the UK and Europe. This has had a great impact and an influence throughout the years, in particular the 1939-45 war and all that it implied for Jews in UK. The tiny distance of 21 miles, which separate these islands from the continent of Europe, has had many effects. Perhaps most importantly as a legacy of the Holocaust, it manifests itself as a healthy apprehension of anti-Semitism.

The Anglo Saxon anti-Semitic tradition is found in each class and has a long history. It has been called "the longest hatred." The first blood libel leading to persecution was in England, in Norwich in 1144, with a subsequent one in Lincoln in 1255. The Jews of the city of York burnt to death in Clifford's Tower in 1190 rather than submit to a murderous crowd seeking forcible conversion. The expulsion of Jews in 1290 was preceded by a deliberate drowning of a number of deportees. Even the resettlement was achieved by default and not as a planned invitation to return.

More recently, expressions of anti-Semitism in British society tend to be subtle and diffuse. In a compilation of press cuttings from daily papers and magazines about Victorian attitudes toward the Jews, the vast majority of mentions of Jews are pejorative in the extreme. The publication of Cabinet minutes in the 1940s reveal some shocking language about Jewish people and their propensity to "whine" about their condition (this was in response to reports from Europe in the early days of the Second World War).

Anti-Semitism is ingrained and is everywhere but nowadays tends to be polite, covert, and subtle. Chance remarks are heard at dinner parties. At best, there is an attitude of amused tolerance. Jews are recognised as making a significant and positive contribution to the wider society but are tolerated provided they "know their place" and keep an awareness that "they are not quite like us."

Jews in the UK have therefore been conditioned to believe that they will be left alone if they do not do anything to draw attention to themselves when it comes to facing up to social problems. There is a sense, moreover, that the larger society will approve of Jews as having little involvement around crime, drugs, alcohol, mental illness, and especially domestic violence. In fact, Jews feel that they must be more wholesome and family oriented than the general community. Many Jews, perhaps unconsciously, seek to "pass." In recent years this tendency has lessened but one will still find Jewish participants in trade or professional conferences asking for vegetarian food rather than kosher, or wearing a hat or cap rather than a "kippah" or "sheitel." The British class system, despite denials, is still alive and well in the 21st century. Each echelon has its own way of perpetuating an anti-Semitic view and all of the views impact on Jews and their feeling of identity.

The UK Jewish community as a whole has responded in several ways among which these may be the principal ones: separatism; secrecy (absorbing some of those attitudes attributed to it); and becoming more assertive and sometimes aggressive. In the development of JWA these issues have presented problems, and many Jewish women were inhibited from speaking out about their situation.

In addition, the pervasive (an untrue) myth is that all Jews are wealthy. Even a representative from the Scottish Women's Aid movement in requesting a contribution to a faith booklet about the Jewish religious attitude to domestic violence, expressed surprise that "Jewish woman have a charity when they have so much money."

As far as legislation is concerned, comparatively recently physical abuse of a woman by her partner was not even considered by the police to be assault. The police often dismissed complainants and categorised incidents of this kind that came to their attention as "domestics," not the kind of thing with which the police should or would become involved. The existence of domestic abuse was therefore mainly denied and if women sought help the incidents were hushed up or swept under the carpet. Even if the women wanted to leave their homes and partners there was nowhere for them to go. Private rented accommodation was scarce and unaffordable and local authorities had no duty to help.

As with much social advance, the change in society's perception happened mainly through one person's passion, initiative, and commitment. That was Erin Pizzey, the woman who virtually founded the women's aid movement in the UK and created the first refuge at Chiswick in West London. She was very much a woman of her time. In the UK, the late 60s and the 70s were times of considerable social reform and enabling legislation. Domestic violence was recognized as a crime and for the first time local authorities were required to re-house women who were fleeing from abuse.

The UK now has a national Women's Aid Federation, a voluntary funded organisation with hundreds of refuges throughout the country. Many are properties supplied by or through the social housing sector. Most are secular but there is increasing recognition of the need to cater for women from specific ethnic groups. Domestic violence is the fastest growing crime in the UK and accounts for more than one-quarter of all reported crime. The police receive at least one call every minute in every 24 hours. It took a long time to change police attitudes but there are now domestic violence units in all police forces. The Crown Prosecution Service has become pro-active in prosecuting abusers and has set up systems to protect the women and their children, to help them build up the necessary body of evidence to obtain convictions and to find ways to avoid them having to appear in court.

There is also now media coverage of the problem, which is broadly sympathetic. Earlier this year the BBC had a week-long campaign. Under the title, **"Hitting Home,"** it broadcast TV and radio programmes dealing with domestic violence in all its different guises. It has become acceptable to talk about domestic violence and the wider society has recognised the need to do something about it.

The UK government is preparing a new strategy, currently out for consultation. It is proposing to set up an overall and interconnected strategy involving all the public health, welfare, education, and crime prevention and legal services. The case has been put very strongly that publicity and educational programmes must include signposts to special resources, which meet the needs of women of different faiths and cultures. In the 1980s, the existence of racism in secular refuges was highlighted in a report to the government commissioned by Victim Support, a national independent agency.

Recent research presented at a conference at Manchester Metropolitan University, confirmed the particular difficulties of Jewish women. The average UK woman is abused 37 times before she seeks help. Jewish women are likely to take even longer to report.

Now we turn to a short description of Jewish Women's Aid in the UK. In the early 1990s in London, as part of a training programme, a group of social workers discussed domestic abuse, following a seminar, part of their training programme, given by Naomi Graetz, an Israeli academic and authority on spousal abuse in Jewish law. She drew attention to the discrepancy between the ways in which halachic literature describes marriage and what happens in reality in many Jewish homes in Israel and elsewhere. In the subsequent discussions the social workers identified some warning signs, which they had not previously recognized in families with whom they had been working. They began to explore the issues around domestic abuse by asking the women with whom they worked direct questions about whether they were being abused. Later they widened the scope of their enquiries by devising a questionnaire for colleagues in the Jewish social services. As a result they discovered that in the course of the previous year, twenty women had experienced abuse to such an extent that they would have left home, if there had been somewhere to go. They had never disclosed the violence and abuse to anyone previously. This was felt to be the tip of an iceberg as it was confined to the small client group of the voluntary service agency, only operating in London and hardly used by the strictly Orthodox community. The group of workers convened by their then training officer, set up some further meetings, augmented by other interested women, to discuss setting up a "woman for woman" service within the Jewish community.

A telephone helpline had previously been set up by a small group of women from Leeds in 1985. It was aimed at giving a supportive voice to Jewish women who were affected by domestic violence. The women who operated the line from their own homes were very concerned to preserve confidentiality. The level of cultural and religious denial at the time was so strong, that volunteers publicised the helpline under pseudonyms, for fear of repercussions particularly within the small local Jewish community. With some degree of difficulty the two groups were able to come together to hold a national awareness meeting in 1992, and the national UK charity, Jewish Women's Aid, was launched and became a registered charity. It was decided from the beginning that JWA should be a membership organisation. This preserved the grassroots philosophy and ensured its independence from the "establishment" social welfare agencies. It was open to all Jewish women to become members and elect officers to decide policy and to manage the services and the first official election of officers was held in 1993.

At that stage there was no thought of setting up any service other than of augmenting the helpline pioneered by the women from Leeds. It was determined to make this into a national freephone line, and training was set up for women to be prepared for difficult and emotional calls. It was important that they should be well briefed with specific information about available resources but to be non-directive and non-judgmental and ensure that confidentiality was preserved. The other long-term aim was to campaign within and without the community to raise awareness about and against all forms of abuse in the family.

So initially on a derisory budget furnished from the contributions made by participants, a series of meetings was held to raise awareness and develop training for those able to staff the line. In spite of the diversity and range in the Jewish population and the misunderstandings and difficult divisions that exist, women from every part of the community came forward to volunteer. They were attracted by the topic for a variety of reasons. Generally there were those who had had personal experience of violence and abuse in their own families and those who felt fortunate to have been spared. The range of women who volunteered reflected the diversity in the community and gave a good indication of their ability to value each other and work together.

Seed funding was raised from a public launch and that led to the setting up of the helpline as a freephone national service. Further funding was secured to set up awareness training for rabbis and communal leaders.

On the advice of an experienced worker from the women's movement, an application was made to the Housing Corporation, a government supported body which looks for innovative schemes for housing "vulnerable" persons. This funding was granted on the grounds that a refuge was needed for Jewish women where their cultural and religious needs could be met as well as their need for shelter.

At the present time, our aims and objectives have remained the same and have stood the test of time and use. Awareness-raising, community education and accessible and confidential help for the women who need it are the priorities. JWA is there for all Jewish women and their children (if they have any) who need help because of domestic violence. JWA runs a refuge, a national free telephone helpline and support and counseling sessions. The services, although open to all the community, are currently London-based and there are plans to extend them to other areas of the country where there are Jewish communities as support groups become established.

JWA is still a membership organisation with 750 members to date and these numbers are growing. It is a company limited by guarantee and a national registered charity. As such, the Charity Commissioners require there to be a Board of Trustees responsible for strategic development, prudent use of the organisation's funds and monitoring and review of all activities. There was a steep learning curve for the original founders to learn new language and take on tasks like targeting and performance monitoring, quality assessment frameworks, business planning, risk assessment. They have learned fast and understand the need to evaluate in order to justify the existence of JWA and attract statutory funding as well as grants from charitable trusts and individual donations. Like most charities, income is not guaranteed and non-stop fundraising is necessary. This puts JWA into competition with other Jewish charities, as there are no federations as in North America and other communities.

The refuge is nationally regarded as an example of good practice. It can house up to eight women and twelve children and it is generally full. It is kosher and Shabbat and all festivals are strictly observed. Any Jewish woman, whatever her level of observance, can stay there and feel comfortable. The refuge is the only JWA service staffed by professionals and there is now an Executive Director to ensure standards are set and met.

Volunteers are the lifeblood of all the other services. They have to be members of JWA and accept its guiding values and policies. According to their role they also accept training and supervision. They work on the helpline taking calls from women throughout the UK who have experienced or are experiencing domestic abuse. They offer face-to-face support and counselling to women individually or in groups at drop-in venues or in their own homes. They are on the Board of Trustees and those who are qualified to do so give skilled guidance on a number of specialist issues–housing, welfare, financial management, legal, medical, counselling matters. The volunteers are serviced and supported by a small and committed team of professional staff. Administrative expenses are kept by necessity to a bare minimum.

A model has been set up in the London area to provide help and it is hoped to extend to other areas of the country. The work on a full publicity, education and awareness raising package had to take second place in order to satisfy the need for direct service which seems to have been unleashed over the past few years. JWA is actively seeking funding to develop education packs and to offer programmes for Jewish schools and Jewish University societies. Of course the overall aim is the prevention and ultimately eradication of domestic violence.

CONCLUSION

As JWA is a grass-roots organisation, it has been able to attract the attention of women who need help and who do not feel as stigmatised for saying so as they would perhaps in approaching an "establishment" agency. There have been problems in the setting up of Jewish Women's

Aid. Some problems are endemic to the Jewish community in the UK, including a struggle with anti-Semitic attitudes, covertly expressed and often unconsciously absorbed by vulnerable people. The diversity of the community and the rigidity with which some community leaders and teachers regard domestic matters–and each other–produces difficulties. Tensions even arise from the open-to-all membership policy of JWA and the volunteer base it has generated. All these have proved to be manageable challenges in the light of the explicit and shared value base, the high professional standards and the underpinning of traditional Jewish inspiration and womanly warmth.

In conclusion, the authors record their gratitude to the organizsers of the conference in Baltimore. The authors welcomed the opportunity to hear from other Jewish community activists and envied their ability to attract funding from larger communal institutions. They reflected on their journey home on how interesting it was to see how each organisation represented and reflected the culture and the diversity of their own particular community.

There were many differences but amongst the similarities the one which united us all was the paradox and challenge of working within the Jewish culture, which asserts the importance of secure family life, but also in reality is sometimes blind to the inequalities and cruelty which exist in its midst.

Services for Women and Girls in Israel

Ada Pliel-Trossman

SUMMARY. This article is based on a presentation made at The First International Conference on Domestic Abuse in the Jewish Community–*Pursuing Truth, Justice, and Righteousness: A Call to Action*, sponsored by Jewish Women International and Partners, held in July, 2003, in Baltimore, MD, USA. *[Article copies available for a fee from The Haworth Document Delivery Service: 1-800-HAWORTH. E-mail address:<docdelivery@haworthpress.com> Website: <http://www.HaworthPress.com> © 2004 by The Haworth Press, Inc. All rights reserved.]*

KEYWORDS. Israeli women and girls, domestic violence in Jewish community

INTRODUCTION AND TARGET POPULATION

It is acceptable today in the professional literature to see the differences between men and women not only as biological, but also cultural-social and psychological differences defined as gender.

Intervention by social workers and other professionals is required not only because of women's biological uniqueness, economic, family, and personal dependency, vulnerability, and high rate of victimization, but

[Haworth co-indexing entry note]: "Services for Women and Girls in Israel." Pliel-Trossman, Ada. Co-published simultaneously in *Journal of Religion & Abuse* (The Haworth Pastoral Press, an imprint of The Haworth Press, Inc.) Vol. 6, No. 3/4, 2004, pp. 141-148; and: *Domestic Abuse and the Jewish Community: Perspectives from the First International Conference* (ed: Rabbi Cindy Enger, and Diane Gardsbane) The Haworth Pastoral Press, an imprint of The Haworth Press, Inc., 2004, pp. 141-148. Single or multiple copies of this article are available for a fee from The Haworth Document Delivery Service [1-800-HAWORTH, 9:00 a.m. - 5:00 p.m. (EST). E-mail address: docdelivery@haworthpress.com].

Digital Object Identifier: 10.1300/J154v06n03_14

also because of the existing attitudes related to the status of women in society, in the family and with regard to how women see themselves. Working with women provides the means to intervene on behalf of women who are living in a state of distress and for the advancement of the status of women as a whole in society.

The population of women in distress is quite diversified–ranging from women from high socio-economic ranks to women from lower classes. Women in distress are victims of violence, rape, incest, and sexual harassment. They include girls in distress, battered women, subjugated women, women with eating disorders (bulimia, anorexia and the like), women with fertility problems (pregnancies, infertility, and the like), women with health problems and poverty characteristic to women alone (old age, single parenthood, unmarried, divorced, or widowed status).

Psychological and health problems are influenced by a woman's self-image and sexual identification, which determine to a great extent social stereotypes, on one hand, but are also influenced by these same stereotypes, on the other hand.

Specialization in the area of women requires extensive knowledge and familiarity with suitable and unique modes of intervention for the advancement of women as whole, and for the individual care of women in situation of distress and crisis.

THE VISION OF THE DEPARTMENT OF SERVICES FOR WOMEN AND GIRLS

The Department of Services for Women and Girls believes that women are valuable and equal partners in the Israeli society. We put efforts into strengthening and promoting the status of women by acknowledging that gender has an important implication on their course of life, their exposure to dangerous situations, and to their opportunities. Empowering women shall be done according to their qualities, talents and potential, from their personal, social, cultural, and religious point of view.

The Department of Services for Women and Girls will put all efforts towards ensuring advanced and excellent services for women and girls by promoting specialized therapy for women in social services within local authorities, in community organizations and in social agencies.

The long-term results we hope to achieve are as follows:

1. Women who are economically free and independent.
2. Women with positive self-esteem, sure about themselves and at peace with themselves.
3. Women free from stereotyped perceptions on femininity and other behavioral norms related to women.
4. Women who nurture themselves as they nurture others.
5. Women who are assertive and decisive, who implement their rights as equal persons in society.
6. Women with awareness of their physical and emotional needs.
7. Women who are aware of their bodies and health.
8. Women who are able to achieve to their potential as human beings, as wives, mothers, sisters, daughters, and grandmothers, and live in congruence with all of these rolls.
9. Women satisfied with themselves, their status in the family, at work and in society.
10. Women in key positions who will make social, cultural, and political changes in society.

The interventions and unique tools we use in working with women include the following:

1. Therapy, emphasizing the principle of "Equality between Genders," including:
   a. Empowerment–enabling women to reclaim their sense of control and personal power in everyday situations.
   b. Encouraging women to re-define themselves and extend their professional and personal self-concepts.
   c. Encouraging women to develop positive functioning in deferent roles, and at the same time to suggest possibilities of developing careers and other additional skills.
2. Feminist Cognitive-Behavior therapy–changing dysfunctional schemata that are the product of social stereotypes.
3. Equality as a Therapeutic Tool–Individual and group. The therapist uses, during the therapeutic process, his/her understanding that inequality is a social problem that influences women's self-esteem. The way that he/she works with women's inferiority feelings, low self-image, sense of discrimination, and incompetence takes on a different dimension, and promotes the well being of the woman.
4. Creating the conditions to fulfill the stored potential in women. These include helping with housing, occupational job, occupational training.

The goals of our department are defined as the following:

- Improving the status of women in their own eyes and in the eyes of the family, at work and in society.
- Leading general policy regarding the interventions with women and girls.
- Advancing women and girls who are beset by situations of distress.
- Advancing existing services and developing new services for women.
- Promoting legislation in the area of women's rights.
- Training professionals (social workers and others) in the special skills of treatment and therapy with women and girls.

PROGRAMS AND PROFESSIONAL ACTIVITIES

The Programs and Activities That Help Us Achieve Our Vision and Goals and Which Utilize the Special Skills We Have Developed are Discussed Below:

Shelters for Battered Women

In Israel there are 14 shelters (including two for Arab women and one for religious Jewish women). These shelters serve approximately 700 women and 1,000 children per year. The shelter provides first aid for battered women and their children in order to protect their physical well being and assess their needs. In the shelter the woman receives social care through the social worker, assistance and legal advice by a lawyer, care for her children, and referral for her rehabilitation–either by embarking on an independent lifestyle by means of half-way houses, or independent housing, or by returning home with the continued involvement of the community social worker.

The shelters are run mostly by women's organizations and are supported financially by our Ministry and local authorities. The shelters are receiving 100% budgeting for a fixed basket of services.

Half-Way Houses

Last year there were 22 half-way houses, which represent a second-stage of assistance–between the stage of protection, support, and therapy of the shelters and independent life in the community–still with assistance of social workers and occupational training.

Hotlines for Battered Women

There are about eight hotlines for battered women run by women's organizations and one national hotline, supported by the ministry.

Support Centers for Victims of Sexual Assault

The phenomena of sexual abuse cross the lines of gender, age, culture, socioeconomic status or ethnic group. The public agencies which are trying to deal with the phenomenon are: the police, hospital emergency rooms, workers with young girls in distress, and first and foremost, support centers for victims of sexual assault which were established by the initiative of Grass Root Organizations. Volunteers at support centers are on call 24-hours a day. They accompany the victim during the police investigation, in the hospital, provide moral support, and refer her to follow-up treatment according to her needs and desires. Support centers deal with education and information. The types of referrals are rape, attempted rape, gang rape, sexual harassment, indecent acts, sexual abuse, incest, and adult women who were incest and rape victims in the past. There are 11 centers in Israel (including 2 for Arab women). During 2002, about 9,000 women received support from these centers. Our department supports the centers with the average of 30% from their budget.

The Multidisciplinary Treatment Centers for Women Who Were Sexually Abused

The research regarding post-traumatic stress disorder (PTSD) indicates that sexual abuse survivors suffer from the consequences of the traumatic event or the ongoing abuse. The survivors might develop post-traumatic reactions, with symptoms in different areas: physiological, behavioral, and cognitive.

In spite of the severity of the trauma, there was no public treatment for women who need in-depth long-term therapy. Our department initiated the foundation of two multidisciplinary treatment centers in Israel last year (2002).

The therapeutic concept of both centers is holistic and feministic. It focuses on bio-psycho-social treatment, in order to enable the women to cope with the trauma in a healthier way. The clinical process might include personal, family, or group therapy. The treatment emphasizes not only clinical aspects of treatment. The client's operational needs are just as significant. No woman would be able to go into clinical process if her basic needs are not met. For this reason, taking care of needs such as housing and day care is important as well. The therapists in the centers operate as case managers, for that purpose. The feminist perception is basic in order to influence social change, and promote strength in the survivors. Both centers, Rishon Lezion and Haifa, treat 80 women overall.

COMMUNITY TREATMENT

Local social services: About 8,000 women were exposed to individual or group intervention in 54 local authorities. These include battered women, sexual abused women, vocational training groups, and others. Statistics for those served include:

2,550-battered women

158-sexually abused women

1,500-attended 87 support groups for battered women and empowerment groups

1,000-volunteers were trained in 44 groups to assist and support battered women

250-women attended groups of vocational training

2,000-attended group leisure time activities, enrichment, and empowerment activities in women clubs

Training professional social workers: As of this date our department has trained about 200 community social workers. The training takes place in Bar-Ilan University and teaches specific interventions with women mentioned above. The participants, 99% women, mentioned after the courses that what they learned had enormous impact not only on the way they treat women now, but also on their own personal life. Graduates of the courses continue receiving in-service training for the duration of their work, regarding the various techniques of treating women.

GIRLS IN DISTRESS

Adolescent girls undergo a multi-stage identity crisis on the way to consolidating their identities as women as part of understanding their status and roles as women. According to this perception, right from the start girls are in a situation of "double marginality." Their marginal status in society results both from their being in the transition period between childhood and adulthood, and also from the inferior status of women in most of the societies known to us.

The target population is composed of girls in distress, aged 13-21, who have revealed symptoms of personal or family distress and malfunctioning. These may be girls who have difficulty in forming meaningful relationships, who are involved in family conflicts and have difficulty functioning in school or on the job. They are characterized by running away from home, pregnancies, suicide attempts, sexual promiscuity, and some times use or even dealing with drugs.

The goals of the service for girls in distress are the same as those of the service for women. The service also aims to prevent social situations that lead to distress and initiate legislation in this area.

About 17,000 girls are exposed to a variety of services, including special treatment in the community, clubs, and group work, half-way houses, shelters, out-of-house placement, and pre-Army groups.

All the activities mentioned are performed with the joint efforts of our Ministry, social departments in local authorities, governmental local authorities (police, etc.), and of course, women's organizations and feminist associations.

I would like to conclude with two more activities that are taking place in Israel:

THE INTER-MINISTERIAL COMMITTEE
ON DOMESTIC VIOLENCE

This committee has functioned since 1998 and embraces members of various governmental representatives, including our Ministry of Labor and Social Affairs, Police, Internal Affairs, the Judicial Office, the Rabbinic courts of law, the Army, Prime Minister's office, Health, Education, Housing, Immigration, and the Social Security Institution. Included are representatives of the major women organizations such as

WIZO and NAAMAT. As a result of the recommendations of this committee, the government budget increased on many projects dealing with violence against women, and domestic violence.

TRAFFICKING IN WOMEN

Israel was exposed during the last years to the phenomena of trafficking in women for the purpose of prostitution. The police estimate that there are about 1,000-3,000 women in Israel who work as prostitutes in about 300-400 escort services and prostitution houses.

The victims of trafficking arrive to Israel mostly from the former Soviet Union, mostly from Moldova, Ukraine, and Russia. There are also women from Eastern Europe and South America. The conditions in which the victims work are outrageous, they are forced to accept up to 30 clients a day, they are beaten, raped, and are sold from one dealer to another.

An inter-ministerial committee (in which I represented our ministry) provided recommendations on a number of topics, including more enforcement of the law against dealers by the Police, to the Attorney General and legislative changes.

The recommendation that became a governmental decision was to establish a shelter for victims of trafficking. We are now in the process of establishing the shelter that will be run and supported by our Department, and will offer humane conditions for the women.

The shelter will offer psychological, social work, medical, and legal services to the women who reside there. Legal services will enable women to consider instituting various proceedings, including labor suits and civil compensation suits. An attempt will be made to employ support staff members who speak the languages of the victims.

CREATING CHANGE

The Power of the Rabbinate:
Opportunities for Education and Awareness in Combating Domestic Violence in the Jewish Community

Rabbi Lisa B. Gelber

SUMMARY. Despite what some wish to believe, domestic violence exists in the Jewish Community. Rabbis are in a unique position to educate the lay population and to create communities of support and comfort. Rabbis can share concepts, values, and texts from the Jewish tradition that highlight the sanctity of the individual; they can ensure a Jewish presence in interfaith settings that address the issue of domestic violence; they can speak out to colleagues and community members; they can advocate for and create communities of honesty and trust. When rabbis embrace these opportunities to provide education and

[Haworth co-indexing entry note]: "The Power of the Rabbinate: Opportunities for Education and Awareness in Combating Domestic Violence in the Jewish Community." Gelber, Rabbi Lisa B. Co-published simultaneously in *Journal of Religion & Abuse* (The Haworth Pastoral Press, an imprint of The Haworth Press, Inc.) Vol. 6, No. 3/4, 2004, pp. 149-153; and: *Domestic Abuse and the Jewish Community: Perspectives from the First International Conference* (ed: Rabbi Cindy Enger, and Diane Gardsbane) The Haworth Pastoral Press, an imprint of The Haworth Press, Inc., 2004, pp. 149-153 Single or multiple copies of this article are available for a fee from The Haworth Document Delivery Service [1-800-HAWORTH, 9:00 a.m. - 5:00 p.m. (EST). E-mail address: docdelivery@haworthpress.com].

awareness, they help bring God's presence to those in need of healing. *[Article copies available for a fee from The Haworth Document Delivery
Service: 1-800-HAWORTH. E-mail address: <docdelivery@haworthpress.
com> Website: <http://www.HaworthPress.com> © 2004 by The Haworth
Press, Inc. All rights reserved.]*

KEYWORDS. Role of Rabbi, domestic violence education, awareness,
community, safety, peace, healing

U'fros Aleinu Sukkat Sh'lomekha.[1] We offered these words as we began the service designed to provide a space in which to unearth the pain
of struggle, of loneliness, and of frustration so that we might find healing. *Blanket us within the safety and shelter of your peace.* These same
words continue to sustain me in my work with victims of domestic violence and the communities in which they live.

These are, of course, our communities–our Jewish communities. The
ones in which so many naively believe that domestic violence does not
exist, that Jewish homes are exempt from abuse within the family, that
Jewish women with strong, creative, motivated female role models, like
D'vorah and Miriam, could not possibly stand for physical, verbal,
emotional, or spiritual abuse. Yet, we know that abuse happens. To the
best of our current knowledge, domestic violence occurs in Jewish
homes at the same rate in which it takes place in non-Jewish homes. It
shouldn't happen at all. When we ignore it, we absent ourselves from
the responsibility to care for, protect, and nurture the lives created
b'tzelem elohim,[2] in God's image.

Our tradition teaches, "seek peace and pursue it."[3] Perhaps that is
why God's sukkah is so profound an image of hope and healing. Even
the most temporary and fragile of structures can serve as a haven. Even
the smallest of gestures, of kindness, of affirmation and support may
bring peace to someone's soul. As Abraham Joshua Heschel wrote,
"God is hiding in the world. Our task is to let the divine sparks emerge
from our deeds."[4] Peace does not merely exist; it must remain in the
forefront of our consciousness, so that it might be integrated into our
lives and released into the world.

In 1997, the Silent Witness Exhibit and Initiative came to Washington State. Initiated in Minnesota in 1990, Silent Witness is a visual reminder of the problems of domestic violence and our responsibility to
stop that violence. In 1995, at least 30 women in Washington State died

violently at the hands of their husband, lover, or ex-lover. Washington's Silent Witness Exhibit depicted 30 of these women through life-size silhouettes made of plywood, and painted blood red. Each figure wore a shield marked with the woman's name, age, date of death, information about where she lived, an account of how she was murdered, and the outcome or legal status of the case. A 31st silhouette honored those women whose murders went unsolved or were erroneously ruled accidental. I wish that I could adequately represent the emotion and feeling in the room when those 31 figures were displayed in the sanctuary of the Mercer Island Presbyterian Church. We had gathered, an interfaith community, for an ecumenical service of remembrance and dedication, to honor women who had been victims of domestic violence. Surrounded by members of the various faith communities, domestic violence workers and advocates, state representatives, and clerical leaders from our community, we acknowledged the crisis of domestic violence and prayed for healing and for peace. To this day, I receive notes thanking me not only for the presence of the Jewish community at that gathering, but also for acknowledging the critical role of religious leaders in addressing the problem of domestic violence in our communities.

Going out into the community and making a statement about domestic violence that acknowledges the pain and suffering of the victims, and asserts that this is not acceptable, raises the level of community awareness. As important as it is to make those statements within the context of the larger community, it is just as important to recognize the existence of domestic violence, to talk about it, to learn how to identify it, and to put a face on it, in our own space. With this in mind, the Women's League at my synagogue in Washington held a forum entitled "Shalom Bayit–Family Peace . . . Not in Pieces," and asked me to moderate the program. In my capacity as rabbi, I introduced the speakers and interwove various concepts, values, and texts from our Jewish tradition. Messages about the importance of our partnership with God in creation, the responsibility of the Jewish community to address social ills, the role of the rabbi as a careful pastoral listener and someone who provides direction and identifies resources, and the sense that one's home is to be a sanctuary, a place of safety in which God abides, enhanced the informative presentations of shelter representatives, teen counselors, specialists on elder abuse, pediatricians, consultants on the assessment of domestic violence in the Jewish family, and members of the King County Prosecutor's office. Most powerful was the personal story of a member of our congregation. Her strength and wisdom provided hope, supporting the claim of Rav Nachman of Breslov, ". . . you are never given an obstacle you cannot overcome."[5]

Many people cannot comprehend domestic violence as a Jewish problem, let alone one about which Judaism has something to say. In that evening, it became clear to everyone present that domestic violence exists in our world and in our homes; its victims have faces that we recognize. That evening, it became clear that our tradition has something to say about domestic violence, and we, as a people, are committed to doing something about it.

Opportunities for education and awareness must not be limited to the adult population. Teens need to learn to respect themselves and their bodies, as well as those of their peers. The teenagers with whom I studied in Seattle were remarkably aware of the extreme highs and lows that confront them in relationships during these years of exploration and development. During our weekly meetings to explore healthy relationships, the students talked about the need for balance in their interactions with others and how they counted on Judaism to provide guidance about what it means to make the world a better place. Critical for them, as well, was the knowledge that someone from the community, a rabbi, would take time out of the evening on a regular basis to talk to them, learn with them, and really listen to what they had to say. Forty-five minutes of validation a week, for one semester, and those kids not only developed a stronger sense of self and Jewish identity, but strengthened their bonds with me and with their peers.

One more personal experience, and then I'll conclude. Those of you who know me, and those of you who attended the workshop entitled *A Journey Towards Freedom: Healing Through a Community Seder*, are aware that I had the unique privilege of working with a superb group of women in Seattle, WA to create a Haggadah specifically designed to illuminate the relationship between the story of our people's exodus from Egypt and the individual and universal stories of survivors of domestic violence. The creation of a piece of liturgy highlighting the integral messages of our tradition–we are a people who have faced abuse, and a people who know enslavement; nevertheless, we move forward towards liberation and freedom, towards healing and wholeness–reminds us that Judaism is a living, breathing entity that has relevance in our daily lives.

We are commanded to tell our story. The Haggadah is designed for that purpose. We don't sit around the seder table and read to ourselves. We read aloud the story of our ancestors; we interject our thoughts and our opinions; we remember. We honor our memories, whether they be of the one who told the story who no longer sits at the head of our table, or of the wine splotches in each of our Haggadot. Every memory carries a sacred story. The opportunity to share the communal story of victims of domestic violence, in a setting that exudes love and safety, and clearly represents the blessings of Jewish community, is a gift that is never taken for granted by those who participate. In fact, it is a reminder of our responsibility to recognize the existence of domestic violence, to embrace its victims, and to provide a venue for healing–not just a physical space, but a spiritual home within our Jewish community and tradition as well.

Our tradition teaches, *"Al shlosha d'varim ha'olam omaid-al ha din, v'al ha'emet, v'al haShalom–*our world rests on three things, on justice, on truth, and on peace."[6] As rabbis, people look to us for guidance and example. This is not just the work of the traditional congregational rabbinate. Wherever our journey has taken us, we have a constituency, and that means that we have the potential for influence; we have a forum in which to create peace. Not only must we be mindful and in control of our own power and authority, we must increase our awareness of and sensitivity to the problem of domestic violence and share that with our colleagues and constituents. We must not assume that bright, articulate, independent women cannot be victims, nor that "upstanding" members of our communities cannot be batterers. We must advocate for and help to create and sustain communities of honesty and trust, communities in which we are all accountable for one another. It is up to us to help spread out God's blanket of peace and embrace those in need of healing.

NOTES

1. From the second blessing after K'riat Sh'ma in the evening service on Shabbat and Festivals.

2. *Genesis,* 1:17.

3. *Psalms,* 34:14.

4. Abraham Joshua Heschel, *God in Search of Man: A Philosophy of Judaism* (New York: The Noonday Press, Farrar, Straus, and Giroux, 1955), 358.

5. *The Empty Chair: Finding Hope & Joy: Timeless Wisdom for a Hasidic Master, Rebbe Nachman of Breslov* (Woodstock, VT: Jewish Lights Publishing, 1994), 48.

6. *Pirke Avot,* 1:18.

BREAKING THE CYCLE

Creating a World that Is Safe for Children

Toby Landesman

The future belongs to those who believe in the beauty of their dreams.
Eleanor Roosevelt

SUMMARY. Focusing on child sexual abuse and incest, the author imagines a future time where a safe world has been created and identifies some concepts and actions to help get there, including: (1) changes in language and concepts of abuser and abused, (2) understanding shame and (3) accepting the need to work with the complexity of sexual abuse and incest. The article ends with a list of things people can do to participate in creating a world that is safe for children. *[Article copies available for a fee from The Haworth Document Delivery Service: 1-800-HAWORTH. E-mail address: <docdelivery@haworthpress.com> Website: <http://www. HaworthPress.com> © 2004 by The Haworth Press, Inc. All rights reserved.]*

[Haworth co-indexing entry note]: "Creating a World that Is Safe for Children." Landesman, Toby. Co-published simultaneously in *Journal of Religion & Abuse* (The Haworth Pastoral Press, an imprint of The Haworth Press, Inc.) Vol. 6, No. 3/4, 2004, pp. 155-169; and: *Domestic Abuse and the Jewish Community: Perspectives from the First International Conference* (ed: Rabbi Cindy Enger, and Diane Gardsbane) The Haworth Pastoral Press, an imprint of The Haworth Press, Inc., 2004, pp. 155-169. Single or multiple copies of this article are available for a fee from The Haworth Document Delivery Service [1-800-HAWORTH, 9:00 a.m. - 5:00 p.m. (EST). E-mail address: docdelivery@haworthpress.com].

Available online at http://www.haworthpress.com/web/JORA
Digital Object Identifier: 10.1300/J154v06n03_16

KEYWORDS. Child sexual abuse, Jewish community, children's safety, shame

I dream of a world without violence. When a woman I know described her plan to write a story set in a world without rape I realized I had never allowed myself to even think of that as a possibility. I began to wonder, "What would it be like to be a woman who grew up in a world that had never experienced rape?" For a while, it left my mind unusually quiet and blank. I began to broaden the concept and ask what it would be like to live in a world free of violence. How do we envision, and then create, a world in which it is natural that these violations do not happen–without denying that they have or could happen. How do we create a world where people take a clear stance of zero tolerance of these violations, speak up and provide support, structures, and treatment for those who need it–whether abuser or abused–"What do people have to start, stop and continue doing to create a world that is safe for children?" Following are some of my initial thoughts with regard specifically to child sexual abuse and incest. I hope they will stimulate discussion in your home, synagogue and community–and then action.

IT'S OUR RESPONSIBILITY TO MAKE THINGS RIGHT

In a proposal to The Rabbinical Council of America in the late twentieth century, Rabbi Mark Dratch wrote that community denial about physical, sexual and emotional abuse of children "remains inexcusable because we thereby shirk our responsibility to our children, denying the victims of abuse the safe haven of a caring and nurturing home and school, and preventing them from growing up with the physical and psychological security they need and deserve. It is for this sin of omission that our entire community must give *din vi-heshbon*, a complete and unequivocal reckoning. And it is to protect the bodies and souls of our innocent children that we must speak out and act."[1]

WHAT MUST WE DO?

Changes in Our Language

In a world safe for children, people directly confront problems that arise. Language reflects an understanding that each human being has the capacity to harm another and, when injured, to heal.

A conservative estimate of sexual abuse incidents involving physical contact is that at least one in three girls and one in six boys is abused before the age of 19.[2] Children are most at risk from people they know[3] and yet we use language that portrays those who molest or violate, the "other," a "stranger," someone "different from me and mine." Here are some suggestions and rationale for changing our language and concepts.

(1) Stop using the word pedophile and start using the words: father, mother, bubby, zede, uncle, aunt, cousin, neighbor, friend, rabbi, teacher, and coach. Listen as you say, "A pedophile molested him," or "His father molested him." Can you feel the difference?

The use of the words "perpetrator" or "pedophile" makes it easier to detach emotionally and harder to believe that people we know do these things. Demonizing those who molest children makes it harder to develop and fund treatment and interventions. The truth is that child molesters look just like you and me. They do not show any noticeable pathology. Few have criminal records. Some are community leaders. Some are other children.

Changing our language is one way of challenging our tendency to say incest is something that is done by "them," that happens to "them." Changing our language is *not* intended to decriminalize the act of molesting a child. Those who molest must be held accountable for what they have done *and* given a chance to heal and make amends.

(2) Stop using the word "victim" when discussing someone who has been abused. Use the words child, daughter, son, neighbor, niece, nephew, cousin, student, etc. The word victim is loaded with meaning, feeling, and judgment. It is also somehow impersonal. Try it out. "She was a victim of sexual abuse," or, "Sue was molested." "I am a survivor of incest," Or "My father molested me." Which evokes more compassion, more distance? Which is empowering? Limiting? Of course, anyone who has been molested can refer to him/herself with whatever terms they choose. Even then, it can be helpful to explore the impact of the label chosen.

People who were molested are so much more than victims or survivors. Even the word survivor has its limitations as it forever links someone with his or her traumatic history. There is also the dilemma in the Jewish community that the word survivor is most likely to be associated with someone who lived through the Holocaust. At the end of a presentation to a Jewish audience on adult survivors of child sexual abuse and incest, a woman said, "I'm confused. When you say survivor, you mean of the Holocaust, yes?" No. There are many traumas from which someone may survive. Our use of language can perhaps reflect that better by saying, "S/he was molested, abused, tortured, held captive, etc."

Shame Less, Listen More–Elements of a Child Safe World

> *Know whom you put to shame, for in the likeness of God is (s)he made.* (Genesis Rabbah 24:8)

For children to be safe we need to find ways to guide and teach them without shame, to make it safe for them to talk about any experience as well as to be heard and helped. Shame is something we feel. It is also something we can elicit in others. Shame can be understood as an inner sense of badness. There is legitimacy in feeling ashamed when we do something bad. Healthy shame is about what we did. "I feel ashamed that I did or said that." Harmful shame, however, is about who we are. "I *am* bad." Toxic shame makes us feel there is something wrong with us at the core.

An individual does not have to be molested to experience shame. Even the best-intentioned people sometimes shame children by things they say or do: "You're stupid." "You're ugly." "You're an embarrassment." A look or glance can also be shaming. A child who is consistently shamed is less likely to bring up concerns when someone talks to them or touches them in a way they don't like. They are more likely to learn to doubt themselves, thus increasing their chances of being vulnerable to victimization. Being shamed can also contribute to a tendency to shame and victimize others.

When molested, shame can be profound even when there is someone to tell. Effective and early intervention can lessen the shame. When a child is molested by someone s/he loves and on whom s/he is dependent (parent, grandparent, caretaker, etc.), everything changes. Molesting a child is a betrayal. To the child it is incomprehensible. The younger the child, the fewer skills s/he has to deal with the terror and trauma.

Sarah[4] is the three-year-old daughter of Ava and Sam, a recently separated couple. A grand jury has indicted Sam on charges of having repeatedly molested Sarah. Sarah is a lovely, bright child who flinches if you touch her hair or neck. She never used to do that. Her mother overheard a conversation between Sarah and her seven-year-old son Jason.

In a matter-of-fact voice Jason said, "You're a girl." Sarah shouted, "No. I am not. I'm nobody. I'm nothing."

As Sam molested Sarah, he called her his "girl" and stroked her hair. Rather than be "that" girl Sarah defends herself by trying to disappear–to "be nobody, nothing." Shame casts a shadow on her sense of self, her comfort with her body, and being a girl.

Trauma expert Judith Lewis Herman, MD, suggests that feeling bad about her or himself is a way a child attempts to manage the unmanageable.

> When it is impossible to avoid the reality of the abuse, the child must construct some system of meaning that justifies it. Inevitably, the child concludes that her innate badness is the cause . . . It enables her to preserve a sense of meaning, hope, and power. If she is bad, then her parents are good. If she is bad, then she can try to be good. If, somehow, she has brought this fate upon herself, then somehow she has the power to change it.[5]

There is the shame of the experience of being molested. There is also the likelihood of being shamed when a child, or the adult s/he becomes, risks telling. Those who publicly acknowledge having been molested are often judged as bringing shame on the family, the community, and the Jewish people. Listeners ask, "Are you sure?" In some Jewish communities disclosing having been molested can affect a person's marriageability as well as that of their siblings. While there is growing awareness that these abuses happen, there are still those who say, "Not here. Shhhh. It's a shonda (disgrace)."

Within the general population, fewer than 5% of children will tell anyone that they have been molested.[6] It's not safe to tell. Either people won't believe you or, if they do, sometimes what happens makes things even worse. Some children are removed from their homes and communities and put in foster care. In too many situations, in spite of evidence of the abuse, custody is given to the father who molested his child.[7] Most adults who were molested as children don't tell either.

To further complicate this picture, therapist Thomas Goforth underscores the importance of understanding shame as a warning inside a child that the relational bond to a significant other has been put in jeopardy. This injury to the core sense of self has consequences for future relationships, including a reluctance to share.[8] So, it is internal *and* external judgments that keep children and the adults they become silent.

In *Shine the Light: Sexual Abuse and Healing in the Jewish Community* by Rachel Lev, Rabbi Carla wrote, "when I speak with rabbinic colleagues about sexual abuse of Jewish children, they recoil in horror . . . My openness about my history has hurt me professionally, as if I were not the innocent child." [9] Sherrie says, "I cannot talk about my traumatic experience openly. I experience myself as shameful whenever the 'public' mask slips or comes off. It is not just the need to protect myself from shame–from the humiliation of someone 'knowing.' It is the necessity of protecting my parents from humiliation and shame, even though they are both dead." [10]

Even when disclosure is only within the immediate family, many family members get angry with the person who tells and blame them for "ruining our family" or "ruining our lives." This, it seems to me, is in part fed by our tendency to idealize our families, the Jewish people, and perhaps a fear that if others see our problems they will use them to attack us. In this way, we link our survival as a people to appearing to be flawless. It is also painful to know.

Shaming, dismissive or judgmental behavior can also be found in the offices of doctors, therapists, and clergy. It occurs when they react with shock when people tell their stories. We will of course be saddened when someone tells us s/he was molested or abused. Clients have told me that reactions of "oh no, not you?" or startled or horrified looks on the face of a "helper" did not help.

Clients completing their therapy have told me how relieved they were when I listened and accepted what they had told me. As they spoke of their fathers or stepfathers slipping into their beds at night, of pretending to sleep and of what happened next they saw compassion and concern in me, but because I didn't react with horror, they felt somehow less alone, less freaky. They said that because I didn't look surprised that they knew they weren't the only ones. My reaction conveyed that these things happen to people, their talking about it wasn't going to hurt me and so I could be there for them.

Communities must become places that are safe for adults and children to tell. In the *To Save a Life* video produced by the Center for Prevention of Sexual and Domestic Violence in Seattle, Rabbi Dratch reminds us that telling about having been abused is not a desecration of God (*hillul ha-Shem*) but an honoring of God (*Kiddush Ha-Shem*)[12] In Lev's *Shine the Light*, Rabbi Elliot Dorff writes "*hillul ha-Shem*, far from prompting us to try to hide the abuse that is going on among us, should motivate us instead to confront it and root it out."[13]

Lessening the Shame and Understanding the Complexity

We need to do more than provide compassionate listening and opportunities for healing. We need to shift from a tendency to pathologize all who have been abused to seeing them first as human beings. Part of accomplishing this is understanding how we label.

The labeling process starts in the ways we view children who were abused. We create lists that announce, "these are signs of possible abuse in children." These lists are slanted towards identifying problems children may demonstrate such as trouble in school, acting out, problems with learning, with drugs. These equate having been abused with being dysfunctional in anti-social ways. Sometimes that's true. Sometimes it's not. It's possible to be wounded by trauma and highly functional.

I worked as a high school social worker for several years. A number of the girl students were being molested. They were bright, good students, active in lots of clubs, physically healthy, attractive, with good friendships. None of these girls told me about the abuse until they were out of school or married. Why? They said they knew I would have to report it and they did not want to lose their friendships and supports. All the Jewish women in my private practice who were molested as children were high achievers. Criteria on the lists I have seen wouldn't have applied to them.

In other lists, we identify signs to warn us that someone might be an abuser. Do they work? Not well. I think coming up with those lists is a way of trying to allay our anxiety that some people are abusive and that we do not often recognize them. Lists are an oversimplification, which lead some to conclude, "Well, I don't see that in my kids, my family, my friends–so I can put this aside." Oversimplification serves denial.

Many individuals who have survived trauma deserve to be seen as heroes and heroines in their own life stories and potential valued experts and resources in our communities. As author Rachel Lev writes in *Shine the Light: Sexual Abuse and Healing in the Jewish Community:*

> There is nothing good about having been traumatized. Yet, to the extent that people learn and grow from their experiences they have that knowledge to share with others–and not just those who have suffered from the same things. As an activist for peace and safety in Jewish lives reminded me, "Survivors who are healing are not just takers, not just depositories for kindness. They are people whose work to heal forces a deepening of who they are. That depth is a gift to the community. Their depth of character and experience

can be shared and often is, just by virtue of their being who they are. Communities benefit from survivors because they have survived–not despite the fact."

Survivors can be asked to share their knowledge and experience regarding what was done to them and how they heal. They can be invited to be part of planning groups, including those related to prevention or developing healing rituals or services.

Beyond what people can bring to a community, people have a need to be a part of the community. When people define you by what was done to you as a child, see you as defective or wounded, feel sorry for you, the very connection you seek as simply a member of the community is withheld. Jane is a forty-year-old therapist in private practice, a dynamic wife and mother of three young children and the daughter of parents who survived the Holocaust. She was molested by her brother for a number of years and nearly raped by her father's friend when she was ten years old. Each and all of these experiences influence her and yet it is not very often safe to openly acknowledge having been molested or nearly raped. There are many places she can talk about giving birth and the time her appendix ruptured but not about how being molested by her brother influenced how she felt when first breastfeeding her son. We need to explore the impact on individuals and a community when people have to keep silent about significant experiences in their lives. How can we learn from something or change it if it is concealed?

In addition to making our language less pejorative, perhaps shame could be lessened by more religious and lay leaders telling their own stories. What might happen if they said in sermons, meetings, and conferences, "I was molested as a child?" How can we make our communities safe for them to tell, as well?

Learn to Work with the Complexity

Creating a world that is safe for children requires accepting the complexity of abuse and its eradication, as well as all that we don't know and the anxiety that brings. When people ask what they can do to protect themselves or their children, I believe we have to offer something different from lists.

We need to support and teach parents and others who care for children so they can support and teach children about healthy and unhealthy language and actions, children's right to say "no" to unwanted touch as well as where and how to get help. Programs such as Good-Touch/Bad-

Touch® can be helpful[14] but they are not enough. To whom can children go when they are being harmed at home? Too many prevention programs emphasize teaching a child to say "no," encouraging them to keep telling until someone believes them and helps. Can a three-year-old realistically do that? More emphasis on the responsibility of adults to protect children is needed as well as networks of support to help them fulfill their responsibilities. It needs to be okay, in fact, the right thing to do, to confront someone who is harming another.

We protect ourselves and those we love by listening, by learning and discussing, by practicing the values on which healthy relationships are built–respect, compassion, responsibility. We develop ways to talk about our bodies and healthy sexuality without shame. Friends, family, and religious leaders provide safe places for people to tell. We work to stop shaming each other. We confront those who believe and teach that they and their children are somehow entitled, privileged, better than others–that the rules and values of being a *mensch* (good person)[15] don't apply to them. We affirm that no profession or position can be immune from scrutiny and accountability when it comes to abusive behavior of any kind. Mothers and rabbis, teachers and scholars, philanthropists, and inspirational leaders can be people who molest and/or were molested. This is part of the complex picture. Creating a world that is safe for children and for all of us requires understanding about how molesting a child can affect him/her. This too is complex. The impact of molestation depends on the child's age and stage of development, his/her relationship with their abuser, the severity and frequency of the abuse, the availability and significance of loving people in her/his life, whether there was anyone to tell and what they did once they were told. And much more. We like to think that children are resilient. Trauma expert Dr. Bruce Perry tells us children are adaptive, not resilient.[16] While acknowledging the impact incest and child sexual abuse may have on an individual, we must also hold hope for healing for anyone involved in the tragedy of molestation.

Reading and listening to the stories of those who were molested or who molest can help humanize our discussions. Providing venues for the display of their artistic expressions can also facilitate our connection to the range of human emotion abusers and abused experience. Grounded in the complexity of what happens and its impact we are more likely to find solutions that work.

While there continue to be needs for specialized services for adults molested as children, adults in abusive relationships, abused children and those who abuse, it is essential that there be more coordination and cooperation among those who plan and provide these services. The better we understand the commonalities and differences in their experiences, the overlap and interplay of adult and child abuse, the sooner we will end people's suffering.

A VISION OF THE FUTURE

I picture children living in a safe world as confident and self-possessed, their faces free from unnecessary fear (except perhaps when watching a scary movie, or seeing a humongous bug). Free from the terror of abuse, they explore the world within them and around them.

In safe and healthy homes and communities, children are raised with a sense of responsibility for the well being of others, and know the rules apply to everyone, including them. From what I have seen, those who molest feel entitled to control and coerce others even as they may internally feel powerlessness and pain. Providing tomorrow's children with boundaried and abundant love and guidance will enable them to grow into adolescents and adults who will improve our world in small and big ways (*Tikkun Olam*).

Hazing of high school and college students will stop because people will recognize and honor that we are each created in the image of the divine (*b'tzelem elohim*). Teen girls traveling with Jewish youth groups to Israel will no longer be raped by boys on their trip. Grade school boys traveling to camp won't be molested by their counselors. And, if any of these happen, parents and community will confront those involved, hold them accountable (*tzedek*) and be sure those who have been harmed receive the support and help they need.[17]

SOME ACTIONS TO HELP CREATE A CHILD SAFE WORLD[18]

Given the complexity of child sexual abuse and incest and the context within which they occur, there are many actions that can contribute to their prevention and healing. Work is needed in our individual, familial and communal lives. Trauma expert Dr. Judith Lewis Herman identifies (a) creating safety, (b) remembrance and mourning, and (c) reconnection as stages of recovery from trauma.[19] We need to ask what is available in our community to allow each of these to occur. What is needed? What role can we play? Do synagogues and Jewish organizations have policies that establish a commitment to creating a safe community and taking action when safety is threatened or violated by those within the community, as well as outsiders?[20]

To create a world safe for children, we each need to identify (a) what we want to create and (b) how we will participate in making it happen. What can we each stop, start, and continue doing to create a world that is safe for us all?

I hope to help create a world that is safe for children through writing and work I am doing with a creative director to build and/or strengthen connections within communities. We are going into synagogues, churches and community groups to gather stories of who they are and who they have been. Working first to create a safe space, we then gather stories from individuals and/or in groups–teens and seniors, men and women, religious and lay members. Community members, congregants, and staff are involved in every aspect of the process including the themes around which we gather stories. These stories can be used in a variety of ways to open up discussion and build connection. They can be written up or used to create a performance piece (readings or plays). The process gives people an experience of being truly heard. This healthy connecting strengthens a sense of belonging and can help people be whole, whether or not there is trauma in their history. Sharing who we are through story can enrich our lives.

Following is a list of projects that can contribute to building a whole, healthy and safe community. They are numbered, but not ranked. Each individual and community must choose what is the next step.

(1). Help children grow up respecting themselves and others through education and modeling by parents, teachers, physicians, rabbis, etc. This requires education and support of these caretakers on how best to accomplish this and their responsibility, including the healing of their own wounds.

(2). Create a paradigm-shifting team to build a working image of a child-safe world.

(3). Expect and support rabbis and Jewish educators to take a stand on these issues.

(4). Establish communication and coordination of domestic violence and child sexual abuse services.

(5). Implement prevention programs for children and adults based on research of what is effective.

(6). Raise money to fund prevention and healing programs.

(7). Create videotapes and materials for awareness raising and healing.

(8). Identify or create healing rituals, for a range of problems people face, and specifically for those who experience sexual abuse or incest.

(9). Gather statistics on sexual abuse and incest in our Jewish communities.

(10). Find and/or create mechanisms through which to share what we know, what we do well, as well as our mistakes and failures as rabbis, teachers, therapists, doctors, lawyers, etc., working to address these issues.

(11). Audit existing services to determine what is and is not working.

(12). Find ways to work together towards a common goal of peace and safety in Jewish lives, rather than seeing ourselves as competing for limited resources.

(13). Develop a central repositor for literature, and listings of resources, including international, national, regional and local listings sensitive to our diverse community. Marcia Cohn Spiegel, MA, has contributed to this through the creation of a bibliography on sexual and domestic violence in the Jewish community.[21] The Awareness Center is beginning to gather resources and help people network around issues of child sexual abuse in the Jewish community.[22] Editor's note: Jewish Women International lists resources for ending domestic violence in the Jewish community on its website (www.jewishwomen. org).

(14). Improve court and child protective services.

(15). Talk openly about these issues.

Whatever the goal, picture it. Describe how its attainment will look, feel, sound. Make it alive. Together we can create a world that is safe for children and ourselves. Certainly our solutions will have imperfections. Life will always have elements of risk and danger. What we do makes a difference.

When Roberta was ten years old her parents went on a trip and her mother's mother took care of Roberta and her brother. With a look of wonder on her face, Roberta continued, "My grandmother noticed something was wrong and asked 'Is everything okay?' She wouldn't let me say yes. She kept pushing until I told her my brother would come and lay on top of me in my bed and I hated it. She told me she would take care of it. My brother never did it again. She was like an angel representing God." I believe we all can be such angels.

NOTES

1. Rachel Lev, *Shine the Light: Sexual Abuse and Healing in the Jewish Community*, (Boston: Northeastern University Press), 2003. p. 46.

2. In Rachel Lev, *Shine the Light*. These figures are based on research in Canada and the United States. The prevalence data is based on research by D. E. H. Russell, PhD. *Sexual Exploitation: Rape, Child Sexual Abuse, and Sexual Harassment* (Beverly Hills, CA: Sage, 1984). Also, *The Secret Trauma: Incest in the Lives of Girls and Women*, New York: Basic Books, 1986. Also, see Lloyd DeMause, "Universality of Incest," *The Journal of Psychohistory*. Vol. 19(2), Fall, 1991. Statistics on rates of child abuse and neglect are controversial. Where boys are concerned, research demonstrates a prevalence rate ranging from 1 in 6 to 1 in 10 boys. In studies of either gender, different prevalence rates have been found in different samples. Many variables, including the forum and methods in which information are gathered influence the outcomes. For our purposes I am using figures that are commonly accepted. For discussion of some of the variables impacting the validity of child abuse research see *www.jimhopper.com*, PhD Psychologist Jim Hopper's website.

3. *The 1995 Child Maltreatment Report*. U.S. Department of Health and Human Services, National Center on Child Abuse and Neglect (Washington, DC: Government Printing Office, 1997.)

4. Names and identifying information of the people in the stories have been changed to maintain their privacy.

5. Herman, J. L. *Trauma and Recovery: The aftermath of violence-from domestic abuse to political terror*. (Basic Books, 1992), 103.

6. Cory Jewell Jensen, MS and Steve Jensen, MA "Understanding and Protecting Your Children from Child Molesters and Predators." OPRAH.com

7. In cases of child sexual abuse and incest, there are many inequities and problems in the current legal system in the United States. What is publicized in the popular press is often very different than what generally occurs in the courts. For example:

- Child sexual abuse allegations were made in less than 2% of contested divorces involving child custody (Association of Family Conciliation Courts, 1990).
- Richard Ducote, attorney, lecturer and author of over fifteen child welfare laws reports, "After twenty years in family law courtrooms throughout the country, I confidently say that no woman, despite very abundant evidence that her child has been sexually molested by her ex-husband or that she has been repeatedly pummeled by the violent father of her child, can safely walk into any family court in the country and not face a grave risk of losing custody to the abuser for the sole reason that she dared to present the evidence to the judge and ask that the child be protected."
- Given the above, serious consideration should be given to separating decisions regarding child abuse from divorce custody cases. Lawyers, judges, guardian ad litem and other court officials need education and training including clarification of their role and responsibility.
- Kristen Lombardi in "Condition of Abuse," *The Boston Phoenix* (cited by Justice for Children), suggests we ban the use of bogus psychological disorders, such as "parental-alienation syndrome," under the family court's judicial protocol for contested custody cases involving sex-abuse claims (cited by Justice for Children).

8. Personal communication, January 7, 2004.

9. Lev. *Shine the Light: Sexual Abuse and Healing in the Jewish Community*, 30-31.

10. Lev, 35.

11. Dr. Judith Lewis Herman's stages of recovery from trauma are described in her book, *Trauma and Recovery: The aftermath of violence–From domestic abuse to political terror.* Basic Books. 1992. 133-213.

12. *To Save A Life* videotape Center for Prevention of Sexual and Domestic Violence

13. "Jewish Law and Tradition Regarding Sexual Abuse" in Lev, Rachel. *Shine the Light: Sexual Abuse and Healing in the Jewish Community.* (Boston: Northeastern University Press, 2003), 55.

14. Good-Touch/Bad-Touch, Prevention and Motivation Programs, Inc. is a comprehensive child abuse prevention curriculum designed for preschool and kindergarten through sixth grade students. 800-245-1527, e-mail: *GTBT1@aol.com*, website: http://www.goodtouchbadtouch.com/

15. *Mensch* is also defined in the freedictionary.com as "a decent responsible person with admirable characteristics."

16. Perry, B.D., "Incubated in Terror: Neurodevelopmental Factors in the Cycle of Violence," in *Children, Youth, and Violence: The Search for Solutions*, (Ed.). J. Osofsky (New York: Guilford Press, 1997), 124-48.

17. Thanks to Jewish Women International's 2003 Call to Action for the identification of these key principles.

18. I'd love to know what your "world safe for children" looks like and what you plan to do. Let me know at: TALandesman@aol.com

19. Dr. Judith Lewis Herman's stages of recovery from trauma. See footnote 11.

20. Lev, "In Northern California, members of a committee working with the Kehilla Community Synagogue have developed abuse prevention protocols in order to help Jewish (and other) congregations best create environments of safety and healing for all community members. The protocols are designed to be useful for both prevention of, healing from and response to situations of abuse in Jewish congregations." p. 173.

21. Marcia Cohn Spiegel, MA, *Bibliography of Sources on Sexual and Domestic Violence in the Jewish Community* available at: http://www.mincava.umn.edu/center.asp

22. The Awareness Center's website is: http://theawarenesscenter.org

REFERENCES

Dorff, Elliot (2003). "Jewish Law and Tradition Regarding Sexual Abuse." In Lev, Rachel *Shine the Light: Sexual Abuse and Healing in the Jewish Community.* Boston: Northeastern University Press, 55.

Herman, J. L. (1992). *Trauma and Recovery: The aftermath of violence–From domestic abuse to political terror.* New York: Basic Books.

Jensen, Cory, Jewell, M.S., and Jensen, S. "Understanding and Protecting Your Children from Child Molesters and Predators." OPRAH.com

Lev, Rachel (2003). *Shine the Light: Sexual Abuse and Healing in the Jewish community.* Boston: Northeastern University Press.

Perry, B.D. (1997). "Incubated in Terror: Neurodevelopmental Factors in the Cycle of Violence," in *Children, youth, and violence: The Search for Solutions.* (Ed.). J. Osofsky. New York: Guilford Press, 124-48.

Russell, D.E.H., (1986). Sexual Exploitation: Rape, Child Sexual Abuse, and Sexual Harassment (Beverly Hills: Sage, 1984). *The Secret Trauma: Incest in the Lives of Girls and Women*. New York: Basic Books.

The 1995 Child Maltreatment Report. (1997). U.S. Department of health and human services, National Center on Child Abuse and Neglect. Washington, DC: Government Printing Office.

To Save A Life: Ending Domestic Violence in Jewish Families (videotape) FaithTrust Institute (previously the Center for Prevention of Sexual and Domestic Violence) (1997).

Index

BOOK ORDER FORM!

Order a copy of this book with this form or online at:
http://www.HaworthPress.com/store/product.asp?sku=5647

Domestic Abuse and the Jewish Community
Perspectives from the First International Conference

___ in softbound at $22.95 ISBN-13: 978-0-7890-2970-6 / ISBN-10: 0-7890-2970-7.
___ in hardbound at $39.95 ISBN-13: 978-0-7890-2969-0 / ISBN-10: 0-7890-2969-3.

COST OF BOOKS _____

POSTAGE & HANDLING _____
US: $4.00 for first book & $1.50
for each additional book
Outside US: $5.00 for first book
& $2.00 for each additional book.

SUBTOTAL _____

In Canada: add 7% GST. _____

STATE TAX _____
CA, IL, IN, MN, NJ, NY, OH, PA & SD residents
please add appropriate local sales tax.

FINAL TOTAL _____
If paying in Canadian funds, convert
using the current exchange rate,
UNESCO coupons welcome.

❏ BILL ME LATER:
Bill-me option is good on US/Canada/
Mexico orders only; not good to jobbers,
wholesalers, or subscription agencies.

❏ Signature _____

❏ Payment Enclosed: $ _____

❏ PLEASE CHARGE TO MY CREDIT CARD:
❏ Visa ❏ MasterCard ❏ AmEx ❏ Discover
❏ Diner's Club ❏ Eurocard ❏ JCB

Account # _____

Exp Date _____

Signature _____
(Prices in US dollars and subject to change without notice.)

PLEASE PRINT ALL INFORMATION OR ATTACH YOUR BUSINESS CARD

Name	
Address	
City	State/Province	Zip/Postal Code
Country	
Tel	Fax
E-Mail	

May we use your e-mail address for confirmations and other types of information? ❏ Yes ❏ No We appreciate receiving
your e-mail address. Haworth would like to e-mail special discount offers to you, as a preferred customer.
We will never share, rent, or exchange your e-mail address. We regard such actions as an invasion of your privacy.

Order from your **local bookstore** or directly from
The Haworth Press, Inc. 10 Alice Street, Binghamton, New York 13904-1580 • USA
Call our toll-free number (1-800-429-6784) / Outside US/Canada: (607) 722-5857
Fax: 1-800-895-0582 / Outside US/Canada: (607) 771-0012
E-mail your order to us: orders@HaworthPress.com

For orders outside US and Canada, you may wish to order through your local
sales representative, distributor, or bookseller.
For information, see http://HaworthPress.com/distributors

(Discounts are available for individual orders in US and Canada only, not booksellers/distributors.)

The Haworth Press Inc.

Please photocopy this form for your personal use.
www.HaworthPress.com

BOF05